MODERN CREOLE

MODERN CREOLE

A Taste of New Orleans Culture and Cuisine

ERIC COOK

with Jyl Benson

photography by Sam Hanna

FOREWORD BY GORDON RAMSAY

Gibbs Smith

First Edition
28 27 26 25 24   5 4 3 2 1

Published by
Gibbs Smith
570 N. Sportsplex Dr.
Kaysville, Utah 84037

1.800.835.4993 orders
www.gibbs-smith.com

Designed by Sheryl Dickert
Production Design by Renee Bond
Printed and bound in China

Library of Congress Control Number: 2023952556
ISBN: 978-1-4236-6544-1

This product is made of FSC®-certified
and other controlled material.

FSC
www.fsc.org

MIX
Paper | Supporting
responsible forestry
FSC® C153458

This book is dedicated to Robyn Cook. I can't even begin to tell you what she has had to put up with being married to a man who is married to his craft. The restaurant industry is an all-encompassing career. It requires an enormous amount of time and dedication, usually for things you haven't come to learn or understand yet, but requires blind faith for acceptance and growth. Behind every great chef is a loved one who goes to family gatherings and parties alone and has to explain that you are working but you wish everyone well. To those who support the cooks and their unexplainable drive to succeed in this brutal industry, I raise my glass and toast your courage and patience. And to Robyn, I can say only one thing, YOU ARE WONDERFUL.

To all the cooks in the kitchens, in those battleship-gray walls of pressure and pride, I can tell you this. Learn everything you can. Fill your day with work and knowledge. For tomorrow is a new day and no matter what happens, the doors are going to open, with or without you. So make your mark wherever you can.

Be proud of your journey, because success can start anywhere.

CONTENTS

FOREWORD

New Orleans is one of my favorite cities in America. It has an incredible food culture that cannot be matched, and when it comes to chefs in this city, there's only one who stands out for me—Eric Cook. A Marine vet as well as a veteran of the New Orleans restaurant scene, Eric Cook has a vast knowledge of the region he calls home.

I had the pleasure of spending quality time and learning about the bayou from him back in 2020. From the first handshake we had, I knew he was a chefs' chef. His intricate knowledge of the history of Louisiana, its foodways, and its dishes was truly an enlightening experience during our time together. Throughout the pages of this book, I see so much of that knowledge come through. From mouthwatering seafood dishes to amazing meats and desserts, Eric has a true grasp on New Orleans cuisine, and every recipe in this book shows that.

Eric taught me a lot during my time in Louisiana, and those lessons are definitely in every recipe of this book. I'm sure you'll gain a similar knowledge of Louisiana as I did in these pages.

Hope you Enjoy!
Chef Gordon Ramsay
International Chef and Restaurateur

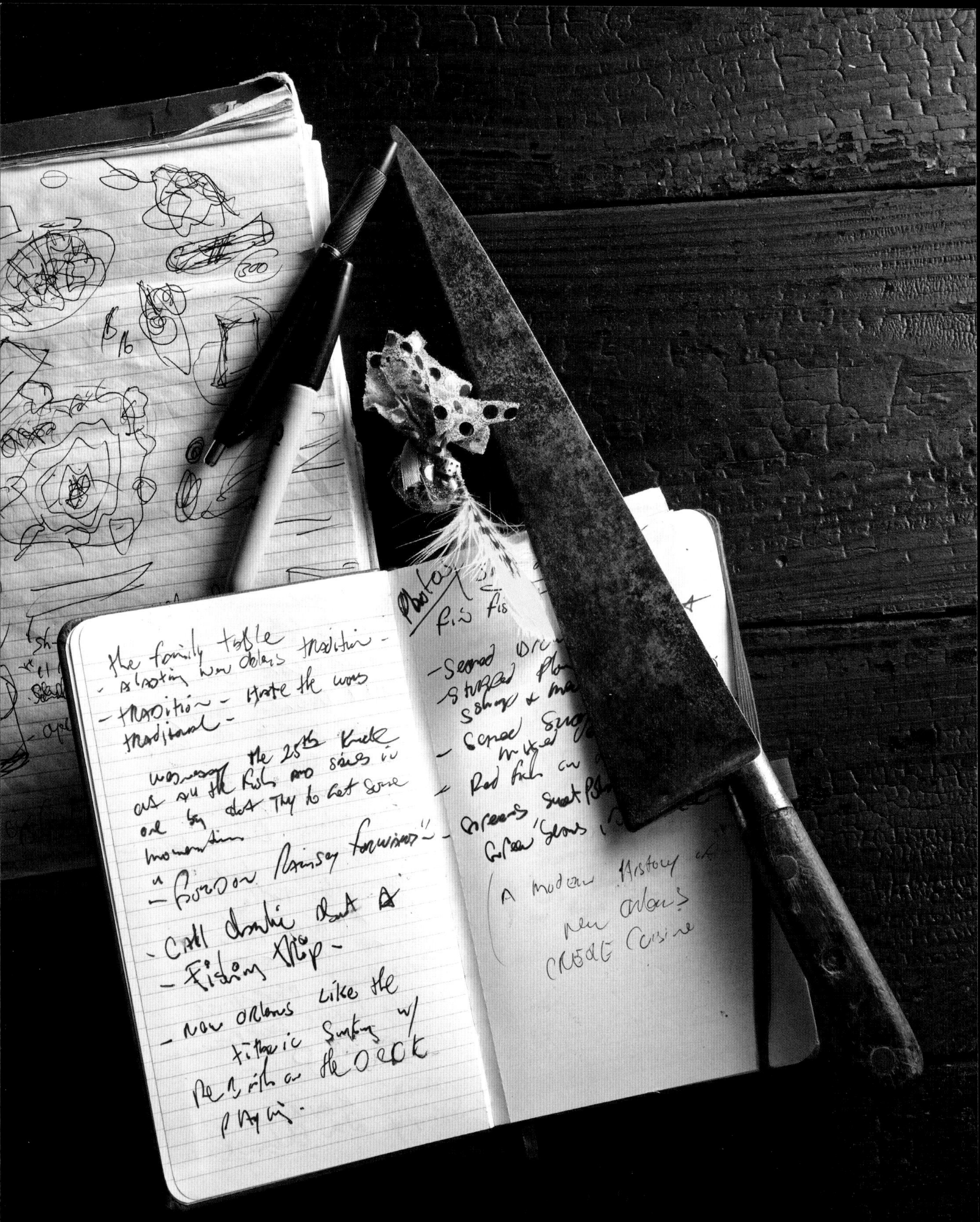

ACKNOWLEDGMENTS

This cookbook would not be possible without the tireless efforts of our entire staff and countless supporters of our restaurants. And to the families who stand behind all of us in this mission to preserve the great heritage of Creole cooking, I offer a heartfelt thank-you. Your passion for celebrating the legacy of family gatherings and holiday traditions that encompass a global melting pot of cultures define our communities as ambassadors to the world.

To Jyl Benson for gathering a team of professionals who provided tireless research and countless hours of editing and rewriting. To my chefs in the restaurants for putting up with all the extra work that we added to the already busy days you have. Darren Chabert, Daren Porretto, and Bradley Marshall, thank you for all that you do every day in the kitchens and in the hearts of our guests.

To Sam Hanna for having the patience to help our vision to come to light and for being able to capture the true essence of the passion we were all feeling on this project, for the late-night phone calls with ideas for photographs, for the ability to see the beauty in simplicity, and for showing us all how the rookie can outfish the seasoned professionals.

To our friends at Gibbs Smith for giving us the opportunity to share our passion for New Orleans and its great history of hospitality and a cuisine like no other in the world. Without your trust and guidance on this book, none of it would be possible.

To all of our friends and family who have supported us on this journey, as it is impossible to list you all, know that I am eternally grateful for the love. This book is for all of you. I hope it brings old friends together and sparks the fire for new friendships to grow and share the passion for our very special cuisine that continues to inspire and keep family memories alive for generations to come.

INTRODUCTION

New Orleans is a city of hidden beauty. Our streets are lined with architecture from a storied and lively past of the many cultures that have, at one time, called this place home. The sounds of music from brass instruments can be heard echoing throughout the streets of New Orleans, and the aromas of a cuisine like no other can take you to a place of red-light districts and speakeasies that once were tucked away and hidden from sight.

Today, we are a community of neighborhoods, seventy-three distinct areas of the city that share a common goal: the preservation of our culture. It's a merging of ethnicity and heritage like nowhere else in the world. At the heart of this is our beloved, shared Creole cuisine. No other American city can claim a cuisine of its own quite like New Orleans can. Like our communities, our cuisine is ever-changing as new people arrive and their ingredients and traditions find their way into the pot. We hold our family recipes close to our hearts while also welcoming the traditions of our neighbors and friends as we revel together in this place of music, art, and expression. We hold firm to our roots, our souls, and our loved ones who came before us and passed on memorable celebrations that are deeply woven into the fabric of the city we affectionately call NOLA.

Though I was born a Cook by name, I never imagined I would end up making a career out of cooking professionally. Growing up in St. Bernard Parish, I was close enough to the city of New Orleans to be exposed to the wild and crazy nightlife that has made it famous over the years, but also far enough away to be able to enjoy one of the most diverse and plentiful wetlands and estuaries found anywhere. Hunting, fishing, crabbing, and chasing wild hogs with my childhood friends were activities that were woven into our DNA by our parents. I went on adventures to Honey Island Swamp with my dad and my brother as a kid, and spent weekends at the camp on the lake with friends, both of which usually involved drinking beers and telling fish stories. Most of those stories were told in the kitchen while cooking up the fish we caught the night before or making gumbo with ducks we harvested that morning.

Simple cooking was normal to us. We didn't have to read cookbooks or recipe cards from our grandmothers. We all spent time in the kitchen with our families on a daily basis. I can still remember standing on a step stool in my mom's kitchen. We had that 1970s crappy linoleum flooring throughout the entire house. I would be peeling shrimp or stuffing crawfish heads for one of Dad's secret recipes, always staring out the window, wishing I was shooting hoops with my friends or riding my bike in the woods around our neighborhood. We had no idea about the great chefs or the grand restaurants that were creating some of the best cuisine in the world just a few minutes away. We were just helping out with dinner. It was a chore and nothing else. It was just what you did as a young person growing up in South Louisiana. We cooked the same way we were raised: simply.

Seafood gumbo with long-grain rice, wild ducks stewed in brown gravy and onions, and fried speckled trout or sac-a-lait in a cast-iron skillet: The food we cooked was sustenance, energy, fuel for the hunt, or the next run into the marsh to chase redfish and flounder. It was a simpler time. Growing up in South Louisiana has to be one of the greatest upbringings you could ask for. Our parents were hardworking and raised a large family on a tight budget, but they would always find the time to share with us the lessons of learning to respect the outdoors and how to harvest its plentiful bounty. That included the importance of preserving it for future generations—a lesson I did not fully understand until I became an adult and had the opportunity to become an ambassador for our culture and our cuisine to the countless visitors who visited New Orleans.

One of my fondest memories of that time is that no matter what we were doing or where we were in our busy day-to-day lives, we always came together at the dinner table as a family, every night. That was our time to stop and catch up with each other. We had a busy household with four kids—two boys and two girls. I was the youngest. We were all involved in just about everything kids could be involved in. Sports all year round, school functions, church functions—the activity list was endless, but we always made time for dinner. I wish we could sit down for just one more dinner like that, with all of us around the table and nothing else in the world going on. The world is a much different place than it was

back then. We have all grown up, moved to different cities, and have our own families now. With work, social media, and endless distractions, it's hard to find time for such occasions. But it's still important to find any time you can to gather with family and friends and just catch up. We may not realize it, but being at the dinner table can create some of the most meaningful moments in our lives and leave lasting memories to be shared for generations. It's the stories and the lessons within them that make the biggest impact.

The "heart of the house" is a term we use in restaurants to describe the very vital part of the team that keeps restaurants moving forward. Front of the house is what the guests see, back of the house is our term for the cooks, and then there are the unseen and unheard—dishwashers, runners, bussers, and everyone who moves around to keep the blood flowing. A flawless dinner service rests solely on the success and execution of this department. It takes a lot of hard work and a bit of stealthy resourcefulness to keep a restaurant running smoothly—and I use that term loosely, as most restaurants run like a roller coaster going downhill without any brakes. But we do it day in and day out because of teamwork. In a home, the heart of the house is usually the kitchen (at least it is in my home). It's the hub for daily communication and small talk. It's the place where the majority of family decisions are made. It's where homework gets checked and schedules made. Growing up, sometimes it was where we determined who was going to confess to eating Mom's chocolate icing she was saving for a special cake. Nonetheless, it's the place where we all come together and set everything else aside to just talk about our day over a meal.

In my family, food was the center of attention for all of us. It was always familiar and comforting, and we ate what was available to us. Some days it was fish from one of Dad's trips with his buddies. There was the occasional roast or ham from Mr. Buddy, the local butcher who ran our neighborhood grocery store called The Chateau. Maybe crawfish were in season, or fresh shrimp for Dad's secret BBQ shrimp recipe that he was so proud of. Red beans and rice every Monday, grits and grillades several times a month. These are dishes that I serve to this day in my home and in my restaurants on a regular basis. They still come from the heart of the house.

Becoming a professional chef was something that happened to me mostly by circumstance. Honestly, it was completely accidental in a very uniquely New Orleans way. If you know NOLA, then you know it's a town where everybody knows everybody. My oldest sister introduced me to a friend of her husband who happened to be the son of one of the owners of Brennan's Restaurant. Up to then, working in a restaurant was not even on my radar.

I joined the Marines when I was only seventeen, and as soon as I turned eighteen and graduated from high school (barely), I left for basic training the same day. Joining the Marines is a calling, but it was more like a scream to me. I wasn't interested in college. As a teen, I was a wild man on the loose with no real direction in my life. I needed discipline and structure, something growing up in New Orleans failed to give me. When I was growing up, the drinking age was five-foot-six, and I was a tall kid. But I had a line of military blood in me. I knew I would excel in the Marines. I was quickly promoted in rank while still maintaining my class clown talents, of course, but in all honesty, I was a hell of a Marine.

Being from New Orleans had its advantages. My mom always sent the best care packages when we were deployed in a foreign country. They usually consisted of Creole spices and lots of booze, which pretty much sums up New Orleans in a box. I spent six of the best years of my life seeing the world and living to the fullest. When my military tour was over, I came back home a little older, a little wiser, and definitely a lot bigger. I recognized pretty quickly that I was a bit lost and even less motivated to join regular society. I missed my brothers in my unit. I missed the structure it provided for me. Then I was introduced to the restaurant business, complete with its battleship-gray kitchens and military-like structure. Before I got into the big restaurant game, I spent several years in the fast casual world of dining. My older brother, who also served in the Navy, offered me a spot in a restaurant he was managing, and as they say, the rest is history.

The legendary Michael Roussel of Brennan's Restaurant is the first person I ever called Chef. To this day he is still an inspiration to me and my career. I could write an entire book about the experiences he gave me and lessons he taught me; some I am still coming to fully understand as I work as a chef and mentor in my own restaurants. He will forever be my greatest teacher, and in a city full of legends, that's saying a lot. He started and ended his career at one restaurant. Forty-nine years of service to his beloved city and its famed Creole cuisine that he loved and shared so generously with all who had the good fortune to come and sit at his table. He ran the kitchen, the dining room, and everything and everyone in the restaurant. He was the first to teach me the importance of knowing everything from the front door to the back. Yes, Chef. That is the response, nothing more, nothing less. If the Chef asks, you do, period. It was my new "yes, sir," the response that I learned in a combat unit in the Marines. You just do it, and you don't ask questions. I soon saw many connections between the military and the kitchen. So I was able to excel in the kitchen ranks as well.

Yes, Chef. That one response, it gave me structure and it gave me discipline again. The kitchen is a place with a chain of command and camaraderie, and like the military, it can sometimes be violent and vulgar. It was just what I needed. That framework keeps me grounded and focused on the attention to detail that separates the great from the average, and that includes your character, not just your skill level. In the past thirty years I have been lucky to have worked for some of the most brilliant minds in the industry. Each one has left an impression on me. Each one has helped me learn my craft. Some experiences were good, some bad, but that is where the discipline comes in. Learn to trust the process, trust those who have come before you, and most importantly, learn to trust yourself. This book shows exactly that—I've learned to trust myself and the hard work that has been put in over my years in this industry. It takes a lot to put yourself out there; the restaurant business is a tough game. You have to be thick-skinned. It's not all perfect white coats and tweezers with pretty flowers and one perfect plate for the camera. It takes patience and the ability to embrace the imperfect and find the beauty in simplicity.

Enjoy these recipes that I have come to love and share with not only my family but the thousands of visitors who travel to our bend in the river, to our Crescent City. Enjoy them with friends on special occasions, or just get into the habit of cooking red beans on Monday. It at least makes it easier to check off the most redundant question of our adult lives, "What's for dinner?" Creole cuisine is for the people, for everyone, everywhere. Throw a party and explore these great dishes that are steeped in tradition and folklore, and don't be afraid to throw your own spice in the pot. That's how this whole thing got started anyway.

I will leave you with the words I often share with those I have had the opportunity and the privilege to work with in the great professional kitchens of our world, "Always be a teacher. Always be a student. In the end, remember that you are just a cook—and ninety-nine percent of being a good cook is just being cool."

So y'all be cool, get cooking, and KEEP EATING CREOLE.

FAMILY MEAL

One of my favorite memories of working in the big restaurants of New Orleans is "family meal," also known as crew meals. When you run a big operation, you must feed the machine, and by the machine, I mean the staff. The soul of every restaurant is its people and the culture that thrives within them. The simple act of providing a hearty meal before the impending doom of the dinner rush or the opening of the floodgates as brunch begins can greatly improve the staff's morale.

It's a chance for the front of the house to sit down and enjoy a few normal moments among fellow table-waiting combatants and recharge for their next shift. Subsequently, at the back of the house, all the cooks and dishwashers usually don't have a chance to break away from their never-ending prep list and tasks needed to get through the upcoming dinner battle. Instead, they learn to eat on the move. Meals usually consist of one of every available protein or vegetable crammed into a vessel that neither hinders your production or draws attention to the fact that you are actually consuming something besides cold beer or whiskey, the staple diet of the inspiring chef. Ask a cook about their life one day. Doing so can make for some of the most enjoyable dining conversations you will ever experience. Family meal is an important opportunity to build allies with the front-of-the-house staff who will ultimately have to cover your ass one day when you make an infrequent mistake in the kitchen. Hell, we got so good at family meal that we would come to work early just so we could have the time to make sure it was done correctly. The part of your day you spend preparing the meal for the staff is some of the most rewarding time spent in the kitchen. It's time you often get to yourself to cook, plan, and execute a meal on your own, a rarity in the world of the busy restaurant.

Jimi Jam, when we worked together at Bourbon House, was the master of coming up with the super spread of items for the staff, usually BBQ chicken with loaded mashed potatoes and cheeseburger meatloaf with homemade pizza and slow-braised turkey necks in brown gravy. Occasionally, one of our cooks would ask to cook something special for the staff and my favorite was those turkey necks.

Big H was what I call a "honcho" in the kitchen, a lead cook, a guy who has the thousand-mile stare from working countless hours and running dinners that ran into the thousands on the weekends. Once in a while he would ask me, "Hey Chef, can I get some turkey necks for the crew?" The answer is always yes, but it comes with knowing that your lead cook, your prep machine, is going to be unavailable for a couple hours, cooking, and that means I would have to pick up his workload or we would spread it out among the sous-chefs to make sure the mise en place for the hotline got done.

But dishes like slow-braised turkey necks and stewed chicken gizzards and grillades are, at their core, the essence of Creole cooking. These are recipes that bring back memories of growing up in the kitchen, as a kid and a young adult—lessons I learned while making a life for myself and my family. They are why I cook the way I do in restaurants and my home, and why I continue to teach and pass on these recipes so that they remain an integral part of the continuation and evolution of Creole cooking. Every dish is a snapshot of a holiday or a meal that evokes memories to someone. I often tell my guests in the restaurant that "brown on brown is the new black." Brown food is not always the most photographic or beautiful food, but you can taste a story in every bite. These are the kind of meals that make people feel like they are dining in someone's home and not in a stuffy dining room filled with strangers. Instead, it feels like you are with friends, sharing a family meal.

COCKTAILS AND YUM YUMS

The South is legendary for its hospitality, and in New Orleans we have perfected the art of throwing a party (for any reason). When people gather here, cocktails are sure to play a role. We like to get every party started with a good drink and a quick bite (what I call "yum yums") to get everyone warmed up. Don't drink? No problem. We also have alcohol-free selections to keep everyone involved in the celebration. You never need a reason to throw a party.

New Orleans has a lot of voodoo nuances as part of our culture. The city was built with very heavy Catholic origins by French and Spanish settlers. In the nineteenth century, enslaved people brought in from West Africa and migrants fleeing Haiti practiced vodou (hoodoo) which over time mixed with influences from Native American rituals and Catholicism, blending to become what we now know as Louisiana voodoo. For most New Orleanians voodoo is not a daily practice or ceremonial religion, but small phrases and meanings are often a part of our language. "Put the gris-gris on 'em" is a phrase we use to send either good or bad wishes to someone, like putting a spell on them. "Juju" is a term we often use for luck. You'll find a lot of references in our music, art, and especially in our cocktails.

GIN BRIGITTE MAKES 1 COCKTAIL

My wife's signature cocktail, the Gin Brigitte, is named for Maman Brigitte, an important loa (spirit) in the voodoo faith. Brigitte is the caretaker of cemeteries and consort of Baron Samedi. She is also associated with the Celtic goddess Brigid, another powerful healer and protector of women. Brigitte is depicted as feminine, sensual, and dangerous at the same time, so it is no wonder Robyn relates to her.

2 ounces botanical gin (Robyn's favorite is Hendrick's)

1 ounce St-Germain or other elderflower liqueur

1 ounce Ruby Red grapefruit juice

¼ ounce lime juice

1 fresh basil leaf, for garnish

Pour the gin, liqueur, and juices into a cocktail shaker with ice. Shake and double strain into a rocks glass with a large ice cube. Garnish with a basil leaf.

CALYPSO QUEEN MAKES 1 COCKTAIL

Celebrating the sounds and flavors of the Caribbean, this refreshing take on spiked lemonade is a must for summertime gatherings. The Tiki bitters adds notes of savory coconut and charred pineapple with brown sugar that makes for an intriguing blend.

½ ounce light or white rum

¾ ounce passion fruit purée

½ ounce lime juice

¼ ounce orgeat

¼ ounce vermouth

3 dashes Tiki bitters

1 ounce spiced rum

Mint sprig and a lime wheel, for garnish

Combine the light rum, passion fruit purée, lime juice, orgeat, vermouth, and bitters in a cocktail shaker with ice. Shake vigorously then double strain into a highball glass with ice. Float the spiced rum atop the cocktail. Garnish with mint and lime.

Gin Brigitte >>

MIDNIGHT SUN MAKES 1 COCKTAIL

Long summer days roll into hot summer nights. Keep the party going with this blend of fresh fruit and Hawaiian black lava salt from the island of Molokai. The deep flavors of charred coconut in the salt add a touch of smokiness and deep-sea salt flavor that is sure to keep the music playing into the night.

1 teaspoon black lava sea salt

¾ ounce Blueberry Shrub (page 30)

1½ ounces orange gin

¾ ounces lime juice

2 ounces prosecco

Fresh blueberries and an orange twist, for garnish

Pour the salt into a small dish. Using a little water, dampen the rim of a rocks glass. Dip half of the rim in the salt. Pour the shrub into the rocks glass. Add the gin and lime juice to a cocktail shaker with ice. Shake vigorously then strain into the glass. Float the prosecco atop. Garnish with blueberries and the orange twist.

LOA SANGRIA SERVES 6

The loa (or lwa) are the spirits of the voodoo faith. They serve as mediators between the living and the dead and between humanity and the divine. Much like saints in Catholicism, or Hindu gods, each serves a special purpose.

1 (750-ml) bottle Chablis

1 ounce apricot brandy

1 ounce brandy

1 cubed Honeycrisp apple

1 sliced pear

1 orange, halved

3 ounces ginger ale, divided

6 mint sprigs, for garnish

Combine the Chablis, brandies, apple, pear, and orange in a large pitcher. Cover and refrigerate for 1 week for best results. For each serving, strain 4 ounces of liquid into a wineglass, add ice cubes, top off with ½-ounce ginger ale, and garnish with mint.

<< Midnight Sun

VODOU MULE MAKES 1 COCKTAIL

This twist on the classic Moscow mule is a fan favorite during happy hour at my restaurant Gris-Gris in New Orleans. The substitution of mezcal in the place of vodka adds a distinct smoky flavor from the process of roasting agaves during production. Depending on the brand, mezcal can also add fruity, peppery, earthy, and vanilla flavors, giving you the ability to mix up your own magic elixir that is guaranteed to make every hour happy.

1½ ounces silver tequila

½ ounce mezcal

¼ ounce pineapple juice

¾ ounce fresh lime juice

2 ounces ginger beer

1 lime wedge

In a copper mule mug, combine the tequila, mezcal, pineapple juice, and lime juice and stir. Add ice and top with the ginger beer. Garnish with the lime wedge.

BLUEBERRY SHRUB MAKES ABOUT 1½ CUPS

For a simple zero-proof cocktail, combine 2 ounces of the shrub with club soda over ice.

2 cups sugar

1 cup fresh blueberries

1 handful fresh thyme sprigs

1 cup vinegar

Mix the sugar, blueberries, and thyme in an airtight container and let sit until the fruit is desiccated and most of the liquid has drawn out, at least 12 hours but no longer than 48 hours. Add the vinegar and let sit for at least 12 hours more. Stir and strain. This will keep refrigerated in an airtight container for 1 month.

Vodou Mule >>

TEQUILA MAMBO MAKES 1 COCKTAIL

1½ ounces tequila

¼ ounce orange curaçao

¼ ounce cayenne liqueur

¾ ounce fresh lemon juice

½ ounce Simple Syrup (recipe follows)

2 dashes Angostura bitters

1 pod star anise, for garnish

Combine the tequila, orange curaçao, cayenne liqueur, lemon juice, and simple syrup in a shaker with ice. Shake and strain into a coupe glass. Top with the bitters and garnish with the star anise.

SIMPLE SYRUP MAKES ABOUT 1 CUP

1 cup sugar

1 cup water

Combine the sugar and water in a saucepan over medium heat and cook, stirring often, until it reaches a boil. After the sugar has dissolved, remove the pan from the heat and let cool to room temperature. Store the syrup in a glass jar with a lid. This will keep refrigerated for up to 1 week.

RIGHT PLACE, WRONG TIME MAKES 1 COCKTAIL

This drink is named after the greatest song by the late musician and icon Dr. John. The epitome of New Orleans music, he mixed jazz, blues, funk, and rock and roll with voodoo vibes throughout his lifetime. We have a commissioned painting of Dr. John overlooking the kitchen in my restaurant Saint John, and his music always gets us in the mood for a good time.

2 ounces bourbon

½ ounce maraschino liqueur

¾ ounce orange liqueur

1 dash Angostura bitters

1 dash tobacco bitters

1 orange twist, for garnish

1 blueberry, for garnish

Combine the bourbon, liqueurs, and bitters in a mixing glass, add ice, and stir. Strain into a rocks glass with a large ice cube. Garnish with the orange twist and the blueberry.

LA VIE EN ROSE MAKES 1 COCKTAIL

The best strawberries come from Ponchatoula, Louisiana, and when they are in season, you will find them on every menu in the city of New Orleans. That includes the bars around town as well. Making strawberry cordial is just like making a simple syrup you would normally make for mixing up your favorite cocktails, and when you have farm-fresh strawberries, you will understand why we look forward to this seasonal sipper all year long.

2 ounces vodka

¾ ounce strawberry cordial

¾ ounce lemon juice

¾ ounce Lillet Blanc

¼ ounce Cointreau

1 fresh strawberry and 1 sprig charred rosemary

Combine the vodka, cordial, lemon juice, Lillet Blanc, and Cointreau in a cocktail shaker with ice. Shake vigorously, then double strain into a coupe glass. Garnish with the strawberry and rosemary sprig.

Right Place, Wrong Time >>

KRÉYOLE 75 MAKES 1 COCKTAIL

This is our spin on a classic French 75, only spicier with touches of Creole seasoning and aperitivo.

1 tablespoon Creole seasoning

1 ounce Peychaud's aperitivo

¾ ounce dry gin

¾ ounce pineapple juice

¾ ounce lemon juice

2 ounces Champagne or sparkling wine

Pour the Creole seasoning to a small bowl. Using a little water, dampen the rim of a champagne flute. Dip the rim into the Creole seasoning and set the glass aside. Combine the aperitivo, gin, and juices in a cocktail shaker with ice. Shake and carefully strain the mixture into the flute. Float the Champagne or sparkling wine on top.

LAVENDER REVIVER MAKES 1 COCKTAIL

2 ounces gin

½ ounce Lillet Blanc

½ ounce lemon juice

½ ounce Lavender Syrup (recipe follows)

1 thinly sliced wheel of lemon, seeds discarded, for garnish

Combine the gin, Lillet Blanc, lemon juice, and lavender syrup in a cocktail shaker with ice. Shake vigorously and strain into a coupe glass. Garnish with the lemon wheel.

LAVENDER SYRUP MAKES 1 QUART

½ cup culinary-grade lavender

1 quart water

4 cups sugar

Combine the lavender, water, and sugar in a saucepan over medium heat and bring to a boil, stirring often. Reduce the heat to low and simmer for 20 minutes. Strain the liquid into a container with a lid. This will keep refrigerated for up to 1 week.

<< Kréyole 75

WICKED ZERO-PROOF COCKTAIL MAKES 1 COCKTAIL

Teetotalers, designated drivers, and our sober friends need good cocktails, too. This is New Orleans, after all. Alcohol is often served at the party, but it's not the only fun part!

2 ounces Ritual zero-proof rum or ginger ale, optional

3½ ounces puréed watermelon

¼ ounce Rosemary Syrup (recipe follows)

¾ ounce lemon and lime cocktail mix

1 small thin slice watermelon, for garnish

Combine the rum or ginger ale, if using, watermelon purée, syrup, and lemon and lime cocktail mix in a shaker. Add ice and shake vigorously. Strain into a highball glass with ice cubes. Garnish with a watermelon slice.

ROSEMARY SYRUP MAKES 1 QUART

10 (4-inch) sprigs rosemary

1 quart water

4 cups sugar

Bring the rosemary, water, and sugar to a boil in a medium saucepan over high heat. Reduce the heat to low and simmer for 20 minutes. Strain the liquid into a container with a lid. This will keep refrigerated for up to 1 week.

GRIS-GRIS OLD-FASHIONED MAKES 1 COCKTAIL

2½ ounces rye whiskey

½ ounce Brown Sugar Syrup (recipe follows)

3 dashes Peychaud bitters

2 dashes Angostura bitters

1 Luxardo cherry and 1 twist orange peel, for garnish

Combine the whiskey, syrup, and bitters in a mixing glass. Stir and strain into a rocks glass with ice. Garnish with the cherry and orange twist.

BROWN SUGAR SYRUP MAKES ABOUT 1 CUP

1 cup light brown sugar

1 cup water

Combine the brown sugar and water in a saucepan over medium heat and cook, stirring often, until it reaches a boil. After the sugar has dissolved, remove the pan from the heat and let sit to cool to room temperature. Store the syrup in a glass jar with a lid. This will keep refrigerated for up to 1 week.

GRATEFUL DEAD MAKES 1 COCKTAIL

2 ounces white rum

1 ounce strawberry cordial

1 ounce lime juice

¾ ounce Peychaud's aperitivo

2 dashes Peychaud's bitters

Lime wheel, for garnish

Combine the rum, cordial, lime juice, aperitivo, and bitters in a cocktail shaker with ice. Shake vigorously and double strain into a coupe glass. Garnish with the lime wheel.

NEW ORLEANS–STYLE FROZEN IRISH COFFEE SERVES 4

4 ounces Jameson whiskey

4 ounces coffee liqueur

4 ounces Bailey's Irish Cream

4 ounces cold, strong coffee

3 scoops vanilla ice cream

2 cups crushed ice

Whipped cream, for garnish

Combine the whiskey, coffee liqueur, Bailey's, coffee, ice cream, and ice in a large blender. Blend on high until smooth. Serve in chilled Irish coffee mugs topped with whipped cream.

Note: For a fun serving idea, dampen the rim of the glass with a bit of water and then dip it into green colored sugar before filling with the drink.

ZOMBI NOG SERVES 10

Our favorite frozen cocktail is made annually to celebrate Mangé Loa, the voodoo "feast of the gods" which coincides with Christmas and Hanukkah. A big batch is perfect in a punch bowl for any holiday party.

4 cups eggnog

3 cups bourbon

1 cup praline liqueur

2 cups heavy cream

Dash vanilla extract

Ground nutmeg and cinnamon sticks, for garnish

Working in batches, if necessary, combine the eggnog, bourbon, liqueur, cream, and vanilla in a blender with ice and process until slushy. Pour into rocks glasses and garnish each with a dash of nutmeg and a cinnamon stick.

New Orleans–Style Frozen Irish Coffee >>

ARTICHOKE BOULETTES WITH GREEN RÉMOULADE MAKES 20 BITES

Think of these little bites as a sort of Creole hush puppy. When I was a kid, my mom would add crabmeat to these treats for holiday parties or special occasions to spruce it up a bit. Frying in a blended oil or vegetable oil keeps them healthier and lighter for guests to enjoy at your next get-together.

½ cup (1 stick) unsalted butter

1 large onion, diced small

1 (14-ounce) can quartered artichoke hearts, drained, liquid reserved

1 tablespoon minced garlic

1 teaspoon kosher salt

1 teaspoon black pepper

½ cup grated Parmesan cheese

2 eggs

2 to 3 cups unseasoned breadcrumbs

Blended oil, for frying

Green Rémoulade (page 208)

Melt the butter in a hot skillet over medium heat. Add the onion and cook until soft, about 5 minutes. Add the artichokes and cook until heated through, about 5 minutes. Add the garlic and cook until fragrant, about 1 minute.

Transfer the mixture to a food processor, add the salt and pepper, and pulse to combine. Add the cheese and eggs and pulse to combine, stopping to scrape down the sides of the processor as needed. Add enough breadcrumbs, pulsing from time to time, to achieve a pliable but not dense mixture. Set the rest of the breadcrumbs aside. If the mixture gets too tight, add some of the reserved liquid from the canned artichokes. Use teaspoons to form the artichoke mixture into balls. Roll the balls in the reserved breadcrumbs.

Heat the oil to 350°F in a deep fryer or Dutch oven. Line a plate with paper towels. Working in batches, if necessary, fry the boulettes in the hot oil until golden on all sides, about 3 minutes. Drain them on a paper towel–lined plate. Serve with Green Rémoulade.

CREOLE DEVILED EGGS MAKES 24 PIECES

12 hard-boiled eggs, peeled

¼ cup mayonnaise

2 tablespoons Creole mustard

4 tablespoons unsalted butter, at room temperature

1 teaspoon fresh lemon juice

1 tablespoon finely minced Italian flat-leaf parsley leaves

Kosher salt

Black pepper

Cut the eggs in half lengthwise. Remove the yolks and rub them through a fine-mesh strainer into a bowl. Add the mayonnaise, mustard, and butter and mix until smooth. Stir in the lemon juice and parsley. Season with salt and pepper.

Cut a thin sliver from the bottom of the egg whites so they will remain upright for filling. Put the yolk mixture into a pastry bag or zip-top bag and cut off a corner. Neatly fill the egg whites by squeezing the bag.

DUCK POPPERS WITH SEARED BACON MAKES 20 BITES

12 ounces boneless, skin-on duck breasts (2 domestic or 4 wild)

10 slices bacon, cut in half

Creole seasoning

8 ounces cream cheese, at room temperature

2 medium jalapeños, cut into thin slices

¼ cup Steen's cane syrup

Preheat the oven to 350º F. Fit a baking rack onto a baking sheet.

Cut each duck breast into 10 thin pieces, or 5 pieces if using wild duck breast.

Lay the bacon halves on a large cutting board. Top each strip with a slice of duck breast. Spread 1½ teaspoons of cream cheese atop the duck breasts. Place 1 or 2 slices of jalapeño over the cream cheese.

Starting at the short end, roll up the poppers and secure with a toothpick.

Place them onto the prepared baking sheet and bake the poppers for 7 to 8 minutes, or until the bacon is crisp, turning once as they cook, and brushing the poppers with cane syrup.

Creole Deviled Eggs >>

SUGARCANE-GLAZED BEEF TENDERLOIN ON TOASTED BAGUETTE WITH HORSERADISH CREAM MAKES 20 BITES

2 (8-ounce) beef fillets

Kosher salt as needed plus 1 teaspoon

Black pepper as needed plus ½ teaspoon

1 tablespoon vegetable oil, optional

8 ounces cream cheese, at room temperature

2 to 3 tablespoons prepared horseradish

1 teaspoon lemon juice

1 French baguette, cut into 20 slices, toasted

¼ cup Steen's cane syrup

Prepare a grill for direct-heat cooking.

Season the fillets generously with salt and pepper. Grill the fillets until they reach an internal temperature of 130ºF for medium-rare, about 5 minutes per side.

Alternatively, you can cook these on the stovetop. Heat 1 tablespoon of oil in a medium cast-iron pan over high heat. When the oil shimmers, add the fillets and sear to an internal temperature of 130ºF, about 5 minutes per side.

Refrigerate the steak until it is well chilled.

In a small bowl, combine the cream cheese, horseradish (adjust to your taste), lemon juice, 1 teaspoon kosher salt, and ½ teaspoon black pepper. Use a wooden spoon to combine until the mixture is creamy.

Cut each fillet into 10 thin slices for a total of 20 slices. Place 1 slice of beef on each of the toasted baguettes. Add 1 teaspoon of the horseradish cream to each piece of steak. Drizzle each bite with cane syrup.

RABBIT LIVER PÂTÉ WITH GERMAN RED CABBAGE ON TOASTED BAGUETTE MAKES 20 BITES

This recipe may sound complicated but is actually an easy way to impress your guests with a savory treat. The application of Cure No. 1, or pink salt, is a technique used in the restaurant to keep pâté looking bright while serving. In the fall, when hunting season is in full swing, I like to use fresh duck livers to keep the snacking going at the hunting camp.

1 pound rabbit livers (or duck or chicken livers)

1½ tablespoons minced garlic

1 tablespoon fresh thyme leaves

6 large eggs

1 teaspoon kosher salt

½ teaspoon Cure No. 1 (prevents oxidation of the liver, available at specialty stores and on Amazon)

½ teaspoon onion powder

¼ teaspoon black pepper

¼ teaspoon garam masala seasoning

1 pound (4 sticks) unsalted butter, melted, slightly cooled

Boiling water

German Red Cabbage (page 168), for serving

Toasted baguette slices or other artisan bread, for serving

Preheat oven to 300ºF. Grease an 8 x 8-inch baking dish.

Combine the livers, garlic, thyme, eggs, salt, Cure No. 1, onion powder, pepper, and garam masala in a blender and process until smooth, scraping down the sides of the blender as necessary with a rubber spatula. With the blender running on high, slowly drizzle in the butter through the feed tube in the blender cap and process until smooth.

Transfer the pâté to the prepared baking dish and set the pan into a larger baking dish or roasting pan.

Make a bain-marie by pouring enough boiling water into the exterior pan to come up to the level of the pate within the smaller pan. Carefully cover both dishes with aluminum foil and bake for about 30 minutes, or until the pate reaches an interior temperature of 145ºF.

Allow the pâté to cool completely. Transfer the pâté to a food processor and process until light, airy, and smooth. Serve with German Red Cabbage and rounds of bread.

MINI CHICKEN BISCUITS
WITH CRYSTAL HONEY GASTRIQUE MAKES 8 TO 10 BITES

These mini bites pack a big flavor with the help of a simple sauce. A gastrique is the simple combining of equal parts honey to vinegar and reducing it over low heat to create a sort of sweet and spicy combination. I love to use sugarcane vinegar and local honey. The addition of your favorite hot sauce can replace the vinegar portion of this recipe to kick things up a bit. Reduce it just enough to get a sticky consistency, but be sure to keep it low and slow on the fire, because you do not want to burn the sugars.

1 cup buttermilk

¼ cup Creole mustard

1 pound boneless, skinless chicken, cut into 2-inch pieces

1 cup all-purpose flour

1 cup cornstarch

1 tablespoon celery salt

1 teaspoon white pepper

1 teaspoon black pepper

1 tablespoon granulated garlic

1 tablespoon onion powder

2 tablespoons Creole seasoning

Blended oil or vegetable oil, for frying

1½ cups Crystal Honey Gastrique (page 100)

1 batch miniature Buttermilk Biscuits (page 158), warmed, split in half

Combine the buttermilk and Creole mustard in a medium bowl. Add the chicken pieces and soak, refrigerated, for at least 1 hour.

Combine the flour, cornstarch, celery salt, white pepper, black pepper, granulated garlic, onion powder, and Creole seasoning in a large bowl and mix.

Heat the oil to 350°F in a deep fryer or Dutch oven. Line a plate with paper towels.

Remove the chicken from the marinade. Add the chicken to the bowl with the seasoned flour and toss to coat. Shake off any excess dredge.

Working in batches, if necessary, fry the chicken in the hot oil until it is golden brown and the internal temperature is 165°F. Drain the chicken on the paper towel–lined plate.

Pour the gastrique into a large bowl. Add the chicken and toss to coat.

Form miniature sandwiches with the chicken and the biscuits.

SEARED PORK BELLY ON COMPRESSED WATERMELON WITH JALAPEÑO DEMI-GLACE SERVES 8

This recipe is great for when those summertime watermelons are available and you are looking to spice up your party menu. If you don't have a vacuum sealer, this dish is just as delicious using fresh-cut watermelon. We use a vacuum sealer in the restaurants to store plenty of portions, and it keeps the melons bright and juicy. You can use a plastic zip-top bag to keep your watermelon fresh for at least 2 days in your refrigerator if you are preparing ahead.

1 small, seedless watermelon

2 pounds skin-on pork belly, cut into 8 (2 x 2-inch) pieces

1 (12-ounce) bottle root beer, preferably Barq's

2 (½-ounce) packages prepared veal demi-glace

1 small jalapeño, cut in half, seeds removed

To compress the watermelon, cut the watermelon into 1-inch-thick slices. Use a 3-inch biscuit cutter to cut the watermelon into 8 rounds. Use a vacuum sealer to seal the watermelon rounds tightly in bags in single layers. Refrigerate for at least 1 hour.

Preheat the oven to 400°F.

Use a small, thin knife to score a shallow crosshatch pattern into the fat side of the pork belly.

Place the pork, scored-side down, in a 12-inch cast-iron skillet set over medium-low heat. Sear the pork belly until the fat side is golden and it releases easily from the pan, about 10 minutes.

Using tongs, move the pork, fat-side up, to a 9 x 13-inch baking dish. Add enough root beer to come halfway up the sides of the pork. Cover tightly with aluminum foil and bake for 40 minutes. Remove the pan from the oven and let cool to room temperature.

Gently heat the veal demi-glace in a small saucepan set over low heat for 20 minutes. Remove the pan from the heat. Add the jalapeño and allow the flavor to bloom for 20 minutes. Remove and discard the jalapeño with a slotted spoon.

Serve the seared pork belly, scored-side up, on top of the watermelon rounds. Spoon 1 teaspoon of the demi-glace over the pork.

FRESH SEASONAL SALADS

Springtime in New Orleans is the most amazing eleven days of the year. When the humidity breaks and the light breeze rolls in off the river, the city comes alive with friends gathering on wrought-iron balconies with refreshing cocktails and salads topped with Creole tomatoes and fresh seafood. Spring really is a very short season down here, but we do get the benefits of garden-fresh greens and some of the freshest vegetables you'll find anywhere. Salads don't need to be the standard lettuce, tomato, cucumber, and ranch. Have fun with the local ingredients available to you. I love to use sugarcane vinegars and stinky cheeses to surprise guests with toppings of crispy fried oysters or shrimp. Composed salads are some of the most popular items on menus these days, so feel free to use these as inspiration, then have fun with designing and dressing your very own creations.

CRABMEAT RAVIGOTE SALAD SERVES 6

I can never make this without thinking of Chef Michael Roussel and Brennan's Restaurant. He did everything old school, and this recipe is about as old school as it gets. I must have made a million of these with him over the years as we prepared for parties, often for the Krewe of Bacchus, in the Chandelier Room. I serve it with butter lettuce, but he always used iceberg. I like to think I'm keeping these old traditions alive but ever-evolving with the modern times.

4 tablespoons mayonnaise

2 tablespoons Creole mustard

1 tablespoon prepared horseradish

1 teaspoon lemon juice

Kosher salt

Black pepper

Creole seasoning

1 large head Boston lettuce, washed, dried, and torn into bite-size pieces

2 large, ripe tomatoes, cored, cut into slices

1 pound jumbo lump crabmeat, cleaned

In a medium bowl, combine the mayonnaise, Creole mustard, and horseradish and blend. Add the lemon juice, a few drops at a time, blending to make a creamy dressing. Season with salt, pepper, and Creole seasoning.

Divide the lettuce and the tomato between chilled salad plates.

Use a spatula to gently fold the crabmeat into the dressing, taking care not to break up the lumps.

Divide the crabmeat over the lettuce and tomato and serve.

DEVILED EGG STEAK SALAD
WITH CAVIAR RANCH SERVES 6

6 (4-ounce) filets mignons (or your favorite cut of steak)

Creole seasoning

1 tablespoon blended oil or vegetable oil

1 tablespoon unsalted butter

Splash of Worcestershire sauce

3 hearts romaine lettuce, washed, dried, chopped

6 pieces bacon, cooked and crumbled

4 ounces crumbled blue cheese

1 pint cherry tomatoes, halved

¾ cup Caviar Ranch Dressing (page 204, see note)

18 Creole Deviled Eggs (page 44)

Preheat the oven to 350°F.

Season the steaks with Creole seasoning.

Set a 12-inch cast-iron skillet over high heat for 2 minutes. Add the oil and heat until shimmering.

Add the fillets to the pan and give each side a hard sear, turning as you go. Remove the pan from the heat. Add the butter and a splash of Worcestershire. Spoon the sauce over the steaks.

Place the pan with the steaks in the oven and cook until they reach an interior temperature of 130°F for medium rare, about 4 minutes. Transfer the steaks to a cutting board to rest while you make the salads.

Combine the lettuce, bacon, blue cheese, tomatoes, and Caviar Ranch dressing in a large salad bowl and toss to combine. Divide the salad between chilled salad plates, and add 3 deviled eggs to each plate. Thinly slice each steak and fan them out on top of the salad servings.

GRILLED FETA AND TOMATO SALAD SERVES 6

1 (8-ounce) block feta cheese

2 tablespoons blended oil or vegetable oil

Kosher salt

Black pepper

10 ounces arugula, washed and dried

⅓ cup Tajin Vinaigrette (page 206)

3 large vine-ripened tomatoes, cored and cut into 8 pieces each

1 Sugar Baby watermelon, rind removed, diced

½ small red onion, thinly sliced

Tajin seasoning, for finishing

Heat a grill to medium-high.

Brush the feta on both sides with the oil and season with salt and pepper. Using tongs, place the block of feta on the grill. Watch it carefully. Just as it begins to sink onto the grate of the grill, use the tongs to carefully turn it over. As soon as it sinks again, pull it off and set it aside to cool.

Toss the arugula, vinaigrette, tomato, watermelon, and onion in a large bowl. Taste and add salt and pepper.

Divide the salad between chilled salad plates. Break the feta into 1-inch chunks and add it to the salads. Top with a pinch of the Tajin seasoning.

CREOLE TOMATOES STUFFED WITH SHRIMP RÉMOULADE SALAD SERVES 4

True Creole tomatoes are known for their dense, meaty texture, low acidity, and rich flavor. They grow alongside the Mississippi River.

2 navel oranges, divided

4 lemons, divided

10 tablespoons Creole seasoning, divided

1 pound large (16- to 20-count) Gulf shrimp, peeled and deveined

6 tablespoons Creole Rémoulade (page 208)

4 large ripe tomatoes

Kosher salt

Black pepper

2 thinly sliced green onions, for serving

Fill a stockpot with 8 cups of water. Squeeze the juice of 1 navel orange into the water, then add the squeezed orange to the pot. Repeat with 2 lemons. Add 5 tablespoons of Creole seasoning, stir, and bring the water to a boil over high heat.

While waiting for the poaching liquid to boil, make a seasoned ice bath. Fill a large bowl or other container with 4 cups of ice and 4 cups of cold water. Squeeze the remaining navel orange into the water, then add the squeezed orange to the water. Repeat with remaining lemons. Add the remaining 5 tablespoons of Creole seasoning. Stir to combine the ingredients. Set aside.

When the water in the stockpot has come to a rolling boil, add the shrimp. Watch closely for the shrimp to turn fully pink, firm, and opaque, 3 to 5 minutes. Quickly remove the shrimp with a slotted spoon and put them in the seasoned ice bath. When the shrimp are fully cooled, drain, then cut each into small pieces.

Transfer the shrimp to a large bowl and toss them with the rémoulade.

To serve, cut the tops off the tomatoes. Cut a thin slice from the bottom of each tomato to allow them to sit flat for serving. Make 6 vertical cuts from the top of each tomato, stopping ½ inch before the bottom. Gently fan the tomatoes open to form a cup. Lightly season the interiors of the tomatoes with salt and pepper.

Use a spoon to stuff each tomato with the sauced shrimp. Garnish each stuffed tomato with green onions.

MIRLITON SLAW WITH CAVIAR RANCH SERVES 6

In Louisiana you might only hear about mirlitons during the holidays. You will often see the classic shrimp and mirliton dressing adorning the tables of Louisiana at special occasions. Also known as the climbing squash or chayote, it has a subtle flavor and is a favorite in many Southern dishes. Some even called it the alligator pear, but don't let the name scare you, it is a light and elegant addition and easy to cook with. It has some seeds in the middle so be sure to cut around the center of the mirliton during your preparation.

2 plump mirlitons, peeled

2 medium carrots, peeled

2 medium parsnips peeled

1 cup chilled Caviar Ranch Dressing (page 204, see note)

Kosher salt

Black pepper

Fill a large bowl with half cold water, half ice. Use a box grater to shred the mirlitons, carrots, and parsnips into the bowl of ice water. Chill until ready to use then drain and dry thoroughly.

Toss the shredded vegetables with the Caviar Ranch Dressing. Taste, and add salt and pepper.

FRIED OYSTER SALAD SERVES 6

Vegetable oil for frying

Seafood Dredge (page 213)

2 egg whites

1 quart oysters, drained

2 heads butter lettuce, washed, dried, and leaves divided

2 large radishes, thinly shaved (if you have a mandoline, use that)

½ cup crumbled blue cheese

Sugarcane Vinaigrette (page 205)

Heat the oil to 350°F in a deep fryer or Dutch oven. Line a plate with paper towels.

Pour the dredge into a large bowl.

In a large bowl, whisk the egg whites until frothy. Add the oysters to the egg whites and toss to coat. Let sit, refrigerated, for 15 minutes.

Strain the oysters from the egg whites. Add the oysters to the bowl with the dredge and toss to coat the oysters thoroughly. Shake off any excess dredge.

Working in batches, fry the oysters in the hot oil until golden brown, about 2 minutes. Drain the oysters on the paper towel–lined plate.

Divide the lettuce between chilled salad plates. Stack the fried oysters, radishes, and blue cheese on top of the lettuce. Drizzle some vinaigrette over the top.

BLACK PEPPER CAESAR SALAD SERVES 6

1 baguette, cut into 1-inch cubes

2 tablespoons blended oil or vegetable oil

Kosher salt

Black pepper

3 romaine hearts, washed, dried, and cut into bite-size pieces

Black Pepper Caesar Dressing (page 207), as needed

Shredded Parmesan cheese, for serving

Preheat the oven to 350°F.

Toss the bread on a rimmed baking sheet with the oil, salt, and pepper until well coated. Bake until deeply golden brown and crisp, about 10 minutes. Let cool.

In a large salad bowl, toss the croutons, lettuce, and dressing. Divide onto chilled salad plates. Top with shredded Parmesan to serve.

MUFFULETTA SALAD SERVES 6

The muffuletta sandwich is said to have roots going back to 1906. Central Grocery in the French Quarter is a legendary place to pick up these treats. Like the po' boy, this sandwich is another example of the deep heritage of the many global cultures that makes New Orleans the greatest food city in the world. The addition of the locally made Steen's sugarcane vinegar puts this salad at the top of my favorite dishes to serve to locals and visitors alike. With the modern resources to have pretty much everything shipped to our front door, I definitely recommend adding these items to your everyday pantry.

1 small head of iceberg lettuce, washed, dried, and chopped into bite-size pieces

1 (16-ounce) jar Italian olive salad

¼ pound mortadella, diced

¼ pound uncured ham, diced

¼ pound salami, diced

2 cups shredded smoked provolone

¼ cup Steen's sugarcane vinegar

12 whole peperoncini

Combine the lettuce, olive salad, meats, cheese, and vinegar in a large salad bowl and toss to combine.

Divide evenly among chilled salad plates. Top each with 2 peppers.

SOUPS, STEWS, AND ONE-POT COOKING

When guests are sitting at the chef's counter at one of my restaurants, the topic of seasons often comes up. Why is the duck off the menu? When is the rabbit coming back? The response is always the same, "Those items are on our winter menu." In New Orleans there are very important seasons throughout the year, none of which have anything to do with weather. There's Crawfish Season, Carnival Season, and Festival Season. These are just a few of the ways we mark our calendars for anticipated menu items and food that only comes around once a year like Mardi Gras king cake and Jazz Fest crawfish bread. However, we don't need a cold front to enjoy hearty dishes like red beans and rice or rich gumbos and stews of rabbit and quail. One-pot recipes have been a staple of the Southern kitchen for generations; they're a great way to feed a big family and keep leftovers for the freezer. I usually joke that weather-wise, there are just two seasons in New Orleans: summer and flu. So don't let the weather stop you from enjoying these recipes year-round. Seriously, we eat red beans and rice every Monday no matter what.

WILD DUCK CASSOULET SERVES 6 TO 8

1 tablespoon blended oil or vegetable oil

2 pounds wild game sausage, cut into ½-inch-thick half-moons

4 pieces thick-cut smoky bacon, chopped

2 cups diced onions

1 cup diced celery

1 cup diced green bell pepper

1 tablespoon minced garlic

½ cup chopped Italian flat-leaf parsley

1 pound dried navy beans, soaked overnight

6 cups Chicken Stock (page 209)

2 bay leaves

1 tablespoon fresh thyme leaves

Kosher salt

Black pepper

2 cups unseasoned breadcrumbs

4 legs Duck Leg Confit (recipe follows)

Heat the oil in a 6-quart cast-iron Dutch oven set over medium heat. Add the sausage and bacon and cook until the fat renders, about 5 minutes.

Add the onions, celery, bell pepper, garlic, and parsley and cook until the vegetables have softened, about 15 minutes.

Drain the beans and add them to the pot along with the stock and the bay leaves. Bring to a simmer.

Reduce the heat to low and cook until the beans have softened and no liquid is visible around the edges, 45 minutes to 1 hour.

Preheat the oven to 375°F.

Remove the bay leaves and stir in the thyme and salt and pepper to taste. Top the cassoulet with breadcrumbs. Put the confit duck on top of the cassoulet and bake for 15 minutes.

DUCK LEG CONFIT

Duck legs or other poultry legs are cured in salt overnight, then submerged in fat and slow-cooked until the meat falls from the bone. Store the legs in the refrigerator in the fat they cooked in. Use the fat to make more confit or to flavor other dishes.

2¼ pounds poultry leg quarters (about 4 duck, chicken, or pheasant legs, or about 2 wild turkey legs)

Kosher salt

2 to 4 cups rendered poultry fat or duck fat, or blended oil, at room temperature

Season the poultry legs generously with salt. Put them in a baking dish, cover, and refrigerate overnight.

Preheat the oven to 300°F.

Wipe the salt from the legs with paper towels and then put them back in the baking dish. Cover the legs with the fat or oil.

Cover the baking dish with aluminum foil and bake until the meat shows no resistance when pierced with a paring knife and the skin has begun to pull away from the bottom of the drumstick, 3½ to 4 hours.

Uncover and cool the legs to room temperature. Press the legs down into the fat. Once thoroughly cool, cover the dish or place them in another container, cover tightly, and refrigerate.

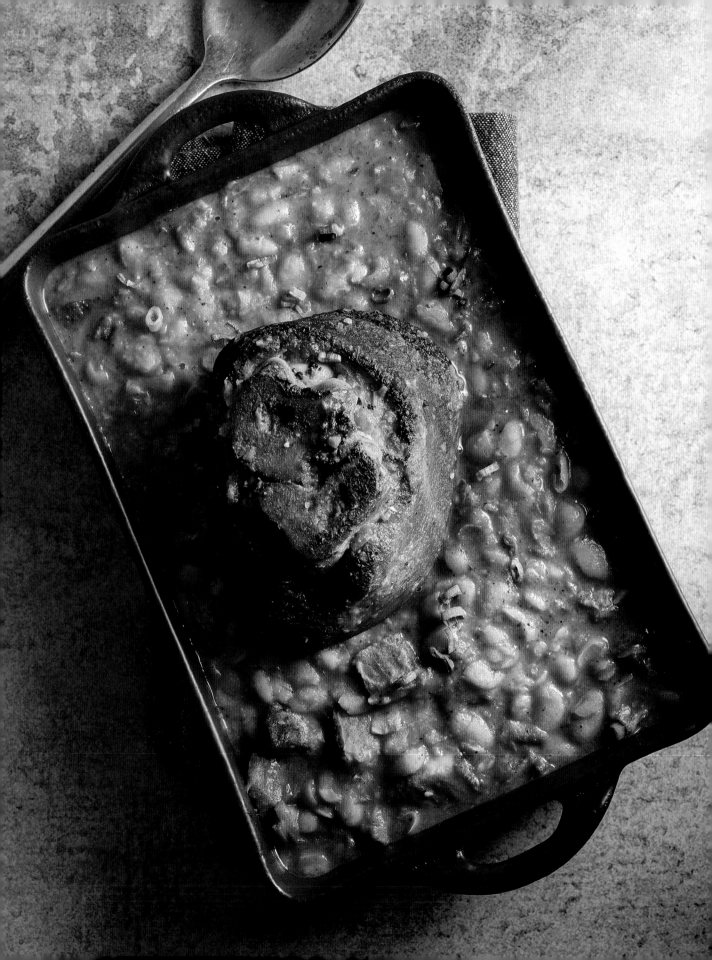

CREOLE WHITE BEANS SERVES 6

Growing up, white beans were right up there with red beans, I tend to lean toward white beans personally. But they both begin with same steps, soaking the beans overnight and building your dish with the "holy trinity." Celery, onions, and bell pepper are the base for countless recipes in South Louisiana, and it's definitely the beginning for many of our dishes in the restaurants of New Orleans. This combination of flavors that provides the cornerstone for our most storied dishes is usually accompanied with chopped garlic and fresh parsley.

This is a great dish to start early in the day and allow to slowly cook while you get the chores done around the house, and it also lets the neighbors know something good is going on in your kitchen. The smell can be intoxicating. Someone should really make scented candles of New Orleans dishes—just don't forget who gave you the idea.

1 pound thick-cut bacon, cut into cubes

12 ounces tasso ham, diced

4 cups diced onions

2 cups diced celery

2 cups diced green bell peppers

1 pound navy beans, soaked overnight, drained

1 bay leaf

1 (1¼- to 1½-pound) smoked pork hock

3 quarts Chicken Stock (page 209)

Creole seasoning

½ bunch Italian flat-leaf parsley, leaves only, chopped

1 bunch green onions, chopped

Cooked long-grain white rice, for serving

Render the fat from the bacon in a cast-iron Dutch oven over medium heat until the bacon is soft and brick red, about 10 minutes.

Add the tasso, stir, and increase the heat to medium-high. Add the onions, celery, and bell peppers and cook, stirring often, until the vegetables are soft, about 15 minutes.

Add the drained white beans, bay leaf, pork hock, and enough chicken stock to cover the beans and bring to a boil.

Reduce the heat to low and cook, stirring occasionally, until the beans are creamy, about 3 hours. Remove the bay leaf and discard. Remove the pork hock, cut the meat from the bone, discard the bone, and add the meat back into the beans. Add the parsley and the green onions and stir. Serve with rice.

MONDAY RED BEANS AND RICE SERVES 4 TO 6

The story behind red beans and rice on Monday is one of the countless culinary traditions we have in New Orleans. Its origins go back to when African and European refugees fled to New Orleans in the 1800s. Local traditions mention that on Sunday we made ham for dinner, and Monday was wash day. Cooking and getting the laundry done at the same time is hard to do, so using the ham bone from Sunday dinner to cook a pot of red beans seems like a novel idea. Growing up, my friends and I would take advantage of this common practice and spend the day going from house to house to enjoy a big bowl of beans and rice from all the moms in our neighborhood.

There are as many recipes for red beans and rice as there are stories of its origins, but most agree that soaking the beans overnight helps in the cooking process and helps reduce the cooking time. As far as the use of pickled pork or sausage or leftover ham, recipes vary from block to block. While pickled pork originated before the time of refrigeration, most folks are using their favorite smoked sausage for seasoning and flavor.

1 pound andouille sausage, cut into quarters lengthwise, then into ¼-inch pieces

8 ounces pickled pork, diced (or diced smoked ham)

2 cups diced onion

1 cup diced celery

1 cup diced green bell pepper

2 tablespoons minced garlic

1 pound red beans, soaked overnight

2 bay leaves

8 cups Chicken Stock (page 209)

1 smoked ham hock

1 tablespoon hot sauce

1 tablespoon Worcestershire sauce

1 teaspoon Creole seasoning

Cooked long-grain white rice, for serving

Combine the sausage and pork in a large cast-iron Dutch oven set over medium-high heat. Cook, stirring often, until the fat renders out, about 10 minutes.

Add the onion, celery, bell pepper, and garlic. Cook, stirring often, until softened, about 10 minutes.

Drain the red beans and add them to the pot. Cover the beans with the chicken stock, add the ham hock, and bring to a boil. Reduce the heat to low and cook, stirring every 30 minutes, until the beans are tender, about 3 hours.

Remove the smoked ham hock. Cut the meat from the bone and add it back to the pot. Discard the bone.

Stir in the hot sauce, Worcestershire, and Creole seasoning. Serve with rice.

MY MOM'S CHICKEN AND DUMPLINGS SERVES 4 TO 6

When I was growing up and it was my birthday, I could request whatever I wanted for dinner and my mom would cook it for me. I always asked for chicken and dumplings. It's not a big-deal dish and it's easy to make, but Mom always made it well and it made me feel good. When I opened Gris-Gris, this was one of the first dishes on the menu. I quickly found out I wasn't the only one who had great memories of it.

A large rotisserie chicken is the way to go here. Just pull it apart and reserve the bones for stock. The dumplings are a treat, but this quick stew is also just fine over rice or buttered noodles.

FOR THE CHICKEN SAUCE

6 tablespoons unsalted butter

1 cup chopped onion

1 pound carrots, peeled and cut into quarters

1 cup diced celery

½ teaspoon tomato paste

3 tablespoons all-purpose flour

1½ tablespoons minced garlic

1 quart Chicken Stock (page 209)

2 bay leaves

4 cups shredded cooked chicken

1 tablespoon fresh thyme or 1 teaspoon dried, plus more fresh thyme leaves, for serving

2 teaspoons black pepper

Kosher salt

FOR THE DUMPLINGS

2 cups all-purpose flour

1½ tablespoons baking powder

1 teaspoon kosher salt

1 teaspoon sugar

1 cup buttermilk

CHICKEN SAUCE

Melt the butter in a large cast-iron Dutch oven over medium-high heat. Add the onion, carrots, and celery and cook until the vegetables begin to soften, about 5 minutes. Add the tomato paste and cook, stirring well, until caramelized, 3 to 4 minutes. Add the flour and stir to fully mix all the ingredients. Add the garlic, stir, and cook until fragrant, about 1 minute. Add the chicken stock and the bay leaves and bring to a boil.

Reduce the heat to low, then add the chicken, thyme, pepper, and salt to taste. Stir and let the sauce simmer while you make the dumplings.

DUMPLINGS

Combine the flour, baking powder, salt, and sugar in a large bowl. Slowly add the buttermilk while whisking, until the mixture reaches biscuit consistency, about 10 minutes.

TO ASSEMBLE

Use a tablespoon to scoop the dough directly into the sauce. Place the dumplings around the pot so they don't clump together. Press them down so they are just under the surface of the sauce.

Cover the pot and reduce the heat to medium-low so the sauce simmers and the dumplings cook. After 15 minutes, remove one dumpling and cut it in half. If it is the same opaque texture all the way through, then it's done. If it is doughy in the center, cook the remaining dumplings for 3 minutes longer. Don't overcook or the dumplings will fall apart.

Serve garnished with fresh thyme.

FAMILY-STYLE POT ROAST SERVES 4 TO 6

I cook this pretty much every time I have a full day off. I get it going in the morning and check on it occasionally when I head in from working in the yard. My family loves when the roast just falls apart. The longer you let it go, the better it gets.

1 (3- to 4-pound) boneless bottom round rump roast

Kosher salt

Black pepper

3 tablespoons blended oil or vegetable oil

3 large carrots, quartered and halved

3 large stalks celery, chopped

1 large onion, chopped

1 cup hearty red wine

6 red potatoes, halved

Warm French bread, cut into slices, for serving

Generously season the roast with salt and pepper on all sides.

Heat the oil in a cast-iron Dutch oven over medium-high heat. When it smokes, add the roast and hard sear on all sides, carefully turning as necessary with tongs. Use tongs to carefully remove the roast to a plate and set aside.

Add the carrots, celery, and onion to the pot and reduce heat to medium-low. Cook, stirring often, until the carrots and onion have started to caramelize, about 15 minutes. The bottom of the pot should be covered in a brown glaze.

Add the wine and use a wooden spoon to scrape the brown bits from the bottom of the pot. Add the potatoes and 4 cups of water and stir to combine. Return the roast to the pot. Reduce the heat to low, cover, and simmer until the meat is tender and falling apart, about 3 hours.

Serve the roast and vegetables with plenty of hot French bread to mop up the sauce.

CRAWFISH ÉTOUFFÉE SERVES 4 TO 6

Crawfish season in South Louisiana is just as much a celebration as any holiday season on the calendar. With that comes opportunities for friends and family to gather for sharing large pots of well-seasoned boiled crawfish and other locally cherished recipes passed down from generation to generation. Étouffée is thought to have been introduced in the 1950s to diners in Breaux Bridge, Louisiana, but may have been around earlier than that. Its name comes from the French word meaning "to smother." Variations of the recipe using shrimp or oysters have come along recently, but all have the same seasonal appeal of bringing friends and family around the table to share the bountiful harvest of a locally sourced delicacy that is like no other in the world.

1 pound Louisiana crawfish tails

1 cup blended oil or vegetable oil

1 cup all-purpose flour

2 cups diced onions

1 cup diced green bell pepper

1 cup diced celery

1 tablespoon minced garlic

½ teaspoon dried oregano

½ teaspoon dried thyme

1 tablespoon tomato paste

2 bay leaves

1 quart Shrimp Stock (page 210)

Cooked long-grain white rice, for serving

Thinly sliced green onions, for serving

Hot sauce, for serving

Place the crawfish tails in a colander and rinse them thoroughly under cold water. Allow to drip dry. Set aside.

Make a dark roux. A large cast-iron Dutch oven is the best choice for making roux because of the way cast iron evenly retains heat. Use a roux spoon or a spoon with a flat end to constantly move and scrape the hot mixture around.

Start by warming the oil in the Dutch oven set over medium-high heat. Slowly add in the flour and start stirring. Stir constantly until the roux is brick-red, 25 to 30 minutes.

Keep stirring while you add the onions, bell pepper, and celery. The roux will be hot. When it has turned into a thick, shiny mass, add the garlic, oregano, and thyme and give it a quick stir. Add the tomato paste and the bay leaves. Stir once more.

Reduce the heat to medium. Add the stock, one ladle at a time, stirring. When the stock is thoroughly blended, add the reserved crawfish tails and stir until heated through. Remove the bay leaves.

Serve with rice, green onions, and hot sauce.

CRAB AND SHRIMP STEW SERVES 6

1 cup blended oil or vegetable oil

1 cup all-purpose flour

2 cups chopped onions

1 cup chopped green bell pepper

1 cup chopped celery

2 tablespoons chopped garlic

1 quart Shrimp Stock (page 210)

6 raw fresh or frozen gumbo crabs*

2 tablespoons Creole seasoning

2 teaspoons black pepper

Kosher salt

1 pound (21- to 25-count) shrimp, peeled and deveined

¼ cup sliced green onions

Cooked long-grain white rice, for serving

Make a roux. A large cast-iron Dutch oven is the best choice for making roux because of the way cast iron evenly retains heat. Use a roux spoon or a spoon with a flat end to constantly move and scrape the hot mixture around.

Start by warming the oil in the Dutch oven set over medium-high heat. Slowly add in the flour and start stirring. Stir constantly until the roux is the color of peanut butter, about 20 minutes.

Add the onions, bell pepper, and celery and keep stirring. When the roux has turned into a thick, shiny mass, add the garlic and give it a quick stir. One ladle at a time, add the stock, and keep stirring as the roux melts down into the hot stock.

Add the gumbo crabs and use a wooden spoon to break them up a bit in the hot liquid. Cover, reduce the heat to low, and cook for 30 minutes.

Add the Creole seasoning, black pepper, and salt to taste. Add the shrimp and the green onions and cook until the shrimp are firm and opaque, about 7 minutes.

Serve over rice.

*Gumbo crabs are whole blue crabs with the backs removed, lungs taken out, and split down the middle, ready for adding to stews, soups, and gumbos.

OYSTER AND ARTICHOKE STEW SERVES 6

Oysters are at their prime in late fall through spring, so this oyster stew is a holiday favorite. The rich texture is from reduced heavy cream, which works well against the brightness of the tarragon. Making it a day in advance allows the flavors to develop while taking some pressure off the host. The artichokes can be blackened at the last minute before serving.

2 pints oysters in their liquid

2 tablespoons unsalted butter

1 cup finely diced onion

8 cups heavy cream

1 tablespoon chopped fresh tarragon leaves

1 (14.5-ounce) can quartered artichoke hearts, drained

2 tablespoons blended oil or vegetable oil, divided

1 tablespoon Creole seasoning

¼ cup sliced green onions

Kosher salt

Black pepper

Drain the oysters over a bowl to catch the oyster liquor. Refrigerate the oysters, and reserve the oyster liquor.

Melt the butter in a large cast-iron Dutch oven set over medium-low heat. Add the onion and cook, stirring constantly, until translucent, 3 to 5 minutes. Do not allow the onions to brown.

Add the heavy cream, the reserved oyster liquor, and the tarragon to the pot and bring to a slight boil, about 10 minutes. Do not scorch the cream.

Reduce the heat to low and simmer, stirring occasionally, until the cream has thickened and reduced by one fourth, about 1 hour.

Blacken the artichokes while the stew is heating.

Pour 1 tablespoon of the oil into an 8-inch cast-iron pan. Spread the oil around with a paper towel to leave a thin coating in the pan. This will ensure nothing will stick. Turn the heat to medium-high.

Transfer the drained artichokes to a bowl. Add the remaining 1 table-spoon of oil and the Creole seasoning and toss to coat the artichokes.

Place the artichokes in one layer in the hot pan and cook until charred, 2 to 3 minutes. Turn the artichokes and char the other side. Set aside.

When the stew has come to a simmer, add the green onions and the reserved oysters and cook until the oysters are plump and the edges begin to curl, 2 to 3 minutes. Season with salt and pepper.

Serve the stew topped with blackened artichokes.

GUMBO

Everyone will tell you the key to a great gumbo starts with the roux. I use equal parts flour to oil. A dark roux takes time and patience, but when done properly, there is no substitute. Stirring constantly and slowly ensures you won't burn the roux, but it also gives you plenty of time to enjoy your company and maybe have a glass of wine or two. Add the "holy trinity" of celery, onions, and bell peppers to stop the cooking process when the roux reaches the color you are looking for. I like a dark fudge color for this gumbo. Cooking the vegetables down in the roux continues to layer on the rich flavors that will win over your family and neighbors every time. Slow and low is the way to make sure all the flavors come together, which is why it usually takes about two hours to make this. Well worth the wait.

CHICKEN AND ANDOUILLE GUMBO   SERVES 8 TO 10

A good dark chicken stock is what I prefer when cooking poultry and sausage gumbo. Fresh local andouille is my go-to for this recipe, and you can use roasted chicken or wild duck when in season.

1 (4-pound) whole chicken

3 bay leaves

½ teaspoon cayenne pepper

1 cup blended oil or vegetable oil

1 cup all-purpose flour

2 cups diced onions

1 cup diced celery

1 cup diced red bell pepper

¼ cup minced garlic

Chicken Stock (page 209), as needed

1 pound smoked andouille sausage

1 tablespoon Crystal hot sauce

1 teaspoon Worcestershire sauce

Kosher salt

Black pepper

Creole seasoning

¼ cup chopped green onions

Cooked long-grain white rice, for serving

Remove the neck and gizzard packet from inside the chicken if it has one, and discard or reserve for another use.

Put the chicken into a large stockpot set over medium heat. Cover with water and bring to a simmer. Add the bay leaves and cayenne pepper, reduce the heat to low, cover, and simmer until the chicken is fully cooked and opaque, about 1 hour.

Remove the chicken from the liquid. Reserve the liquid and discard the bay leaves. Remove meat from the chicken bones and set aside. Reserve the skin and bones for later use in a stock or discard.

Make a dark roux. A large cast-iron Dutch oven is the best choice for making roux because of the way cast iron evenly retains heat. Use a roux spoon or a spoon with a flat end to constantly move and scrape the hot mixture around.

Start by warming the oil in the Dutch oven set over medium-high heat. Slowly add in the flour and start stirring. Stir constantly until the roux is the color of dark fudge, 30 to 45 minutes.

Add the onions, celery, and bell pepper and keep stirring until the roux has turned into a thick shiny mass, about 5 minutes. Add the garlic and give it a quick stir. One ladle at a time, add about 2 cups of the reserved liquid from cooking the chicken, stirring constantly as the roux melts down into the hot stock. If needed add more stock to make a thinner, dark gumbo.

continued >>

Add the cooked chicken and the andouille sausage, stir, and bring the gumbo to a boil. Reduce the heat to low and simmer for 2 hours, stirring occasionally.

Add the hot sauce and the Worcestershire sauce. Season with salt, black pepper, and Creole seasoning to taste. Add the green onions and stir. Serve over rice.

RIVER ROAD SEAFOOD GUMBO SERVES 6

1 cup blended oil or vegetable oil

1 cup all-purpose flour

1 cup diced onion

½ cup diced green bell pepper

½ cup diced celery

1½ tablespoons minced garlic

4 cups hot Chicken Stock (page 209)

2 cups hot Shrimp Stock (page 210)

2 pounds gumbo crabs*

12 ounces okra, sliced

1 pound Gulf claw crabmeat, picked over to remove shells and cartilage

1 pound (21- to 25-count) Gulf shrimp, peeled and deveined

1 pint Gulf oysters, drained (optional)

½ teaspoon kosher salt

½ teaspoon black pepper

Cooked long-grain white rice, for serving

Deviled Egg Potato Salad (page 164), for serving

Make a dark roux. A large cast-iron Dutch oven is the best choice for making roux because of the way cast iron evenly retains heat. Use a roux spoon or a spoon with a flat end to constantly move and scrape the hot mixture around.

Start by warming the oil in the Dutch oven set over medium-high heat. Slowly add in the flour and start stirring. Stir constantly until the roux is the color of dark fudge, 30 to 45 minutes.

Add the onion, bell pepper, and celery and keep stirring, until the roux has turned into a thick shiny mass, about 5 minutes. Add the garlic and give it a quick stir. One ladle at a time, add the stocks and keep stirring as the roux melts down into the hot liquid. Add the gumbo crabs and use a wooden spoon to break them up a bit into the hot liquid. Cover, reduce the heat to low, and cook until vegetables have almost dissolved, about 1 hour.

Add the okra and cook until it softens, about 20 minutes.

Add the crabmeat and the shrimp and stir. Cover and cook for an additional 20 minutes.

If using, add the oysters to the gumbo. Cover and cook until the edges of the oysters plump up and begin to curl, about 5 minutes. Add salt and pepper, adjusting amount as needed. Serve with rice and potato salad.

*Gumbo crabs are whole blue crabs with the backs removed, lungs taken out, and split down the middle, ready for adding to stews, soups, and gumbos.

SEAFOOD

I grew up in Arabi, just outside of New Orleans. It's home to the very first Popeyes Famous Fried Chicken, and just a short drive from some of the world's greatest fishing. Seafood was a constant on the dinner table and at family gatherings. Shrimp, crabs, crawfish, fresh fish, and salty Gulf oysters always filled our table and our bellies. Having fresh seafood available is a blessing. Knowing what to do with it is a birthright to those born in Southeast Louisiana. We pass our recipes and our cast-iron cookware down through generations as family heirlooms. They are part of the traditions and celebrations that bind our people together. Always invest in the freshest local seafood available to you. Invite a bunch of friends over and crank up the tunes of WWOZ (90.7 FM or streaming on wwoz.org), the definitive New Orleans radio station, and "Let the Good Times Roll."

BOILED SHRIMP SERVES 6

Seafood boils are a right of passage for anyone looking to enjoy the best way to experience the freshest seafood found on the Gulf Coast. The recipes are as varied as the local ingredients are abundant. Seasonings for boiled seafood are available in every store in Louisiana. Zatarain's is one of my favorites, but there are tons of choices, from citrus grown south of the city of New Orleans to everything you can think of. This is a great base recipe to get your creative juices flowing. Whether you like your shrimp spicy or just well-seasoned with some lemons, garlic, and onions, you won't find a better way to spend a day with friends creating your very own secret recipe.

2 large lemons, halved

2 navel oranges, halved

2 heads garlic, unpeeled and halved

4 large stalks celery, quartered

¾ cup plus 2 tablespoons kosher salt

2 tablespoons Creole seasoning

2 tablespoons Zatarain's liquid shrimp and crab boil

5 pounds (U-10-count) Gulf shrimp, heads and tails intact

Saltines or water crackers, for serving

Pour 2 gallons of water into a 4-gallon stockpot. Juice the lemons and the oranges into the pot then toss in the juiced citrus hulls. Add the garlic, celery, salt, Creole seasoning, and liquid seafood boil. Bring the mixture to a boil over high heat. Cover, reduce the heat to low, and simmer for 10 minutes.

Add the shrimp, remove the pan from the heat, and stir to combine. Steep for 10 minutes. The shrimp should be firm, pink, and opaque. Strain, dump the shrimp on a larger platter, and serve hot with the saltines.

YASSA SHRIMP SERVES 6

This recipe is like New Orleans–style BBQ shrimp but it incorporates assertive garlic and citrus, along with flavors of West Africa. Serve this with plenty of hot French bread to mop up the sauce.

FOR THE SAUCE

2 tablespoons unsalted butter

½ cup all-purpose flour

¼ cup diced celery

¼ cup diced green bell pepper

½ cup diced onion

2 tablespoons minced garlic

1 quart hot Shrimp Stock (page 210)

1 tablespoon Creole mustard

Zest and juice of 2 medium lemons

½ teaspoon dried oregano

2 tablespoons Creole seasoning

½ teaspoon black pepper

½ teaspoon red pepper flakes

1 cup (2 sticks) cold unsalted butter, cut into cubes

FOR THE SHRIMP

3 pounds (U-10-count) head-on Gulf shrimp

Creole seasoning

2 tablespoons blended oil or vegetable oil

2 tablespoons chopped Italian flat-leaf parsley, for serving

¼ cup thinly sliced green onions, for serving

Hot French bread, for serving

SAUCE

Make a blonde roux. A large cast-iron Dutch oven is the best choice for making roux because of the way cast iron evenly retains heat. Use a roux spoon or a spoon with a flat end to constantly move and scrape the hot mixture around.

Start by warming the oil in the Dutch oven set over medium-high heat. Slowly add in the flour and start stirring. Stir constantly until the roux is a blonde color, about 3 minutes.

Add the celery, bell pepper, and onion and cook until softened, about 8 minutes. Add the garlic and give it a quick stir. One ladle at a time, add the stock and keep stirring as the roux melts down into the hot stock. Reduce the heat to medium-low and cook the mixture until it thickens slightly, about 20 minutes.

Whisk in the mustard, lemon zest, and juice. Add the oregano, Creole seasoning, pepper, and red pepper flakes and mix well.

Remove the mixture from the heat and whisk in the cold butter, 1 cube at a time. Do not add more butter until each cube has melted. The sauce will thicken. Set the sauce aside in a warm place. Do not put it back on the heat or the sauce will break.

SHRIMP

Season the shrimp with the Creole seasoning.

Warm the oil in a large cast-iron pan set over high heat. When the oil shimmers, add the shrimp in a single layer and sear on one side until they begin to turn pink and release easily from the pan, 2 to 3 minutes. Use tongs to turn the shrimp and sear the other side. The shrimp should be firm, pink, and opaque.

To serve, arrange the shrimp on a serving platter and ladle the sauce over them and top with parsley and green onion. Serve with hot French bread.

HOT SHRIMP RÉMOULADE WITH FRIED GREEN TOMATOES AND CHOW CHOW SERVES 6

Blended oil or vegetable for frying, plus 2 tablespoons for searing

2 cups seasoned flour

1 tablespoon kosher salt

1 tablespoon black pepper

4 eggs

1 cup whole milk

⅔ cup Seafood Dredge (page 213)

3 large green tomatoes, cut into ¼-inch-thick slices

1 pound (21- to 25-count) Gulf shrimp, peeled and deveined

Creole seasoning

½ cup heavy cream

⅔ cup Rémoulade Butter (recipe follows), for serving

2 tablespoons Chow Chow (recipe follows), for serving

Preheat the oven to its lowest setting.

Set a 12-inch cast-iron skillet over medium-high heat. Add enough oil to come ½ inch up the sides of the skillet and heat it to 350°F. The oil is ready when a tiny pinch of flour sizzles on contact. Line a plate with paper towels.

In a medium bowl, mix together the flour, salt, and pepper. In another medium bowl, mix together the eggs and milk to make an egg wash. Put the dredge in a third medium bowl.

Dip each slice of tomato in the flour, then the egg wash, then the dredge. Shake off the excess dredge. Working in batches, put the tomato slices into the hot oil and fry, turning once, until golden, about 2 minutes. Remove the tomato slices with a spatula and place them on the paper towel–lined plate to drain. Put the tomatoes into the oven while you sear the shrimp.

Drain the oil from the skillet and wipe it out with a paper towel.

Season the shrimp with Creole seasoning.

Warm 2 tablespoons of oil in the skillet set over medium heat. When the oil shimmers, add the shrimp in a single layer and sear on one side until they release easily from the pan, 1 to 2 minutes. Use tongs to turn the shrimp and sear the other side. The shrimp should be firm and opaque.

Remove the shrimp and set aside.

Do not wipe the skillet. Add the heavy cream to the hot skillet. Use a wooden spoon to scrape up the browned bits. Add the Rémoulade Butter and stir until it has melted.

Serve the shrimp on top of the fried tomatoes. Top with butter sauce and garnish with Chow Chow on the side.

continued >>

RÉMOULADE BUTTER MAKES ABOUT ¾ CUP

Our own invention. A flavor bomb for anything—steak, chicken, pork, or seafood.

½ cup (1 stick) unsalted butter, softened

1 medium stalk celery, finely chopped

1 tablespoon prepared horseradish

1 tablespoon Creole mustard

2 tablespoons chopped green onion

Leaves from ½ bunch Italian flat-leaf parsley, chopped

1 teaspoon Creole seasoning

¼ teaspoon celery salt

¼ teaspoon paprika

Use an electric mixer to whip the butter until it is aerated and slightly lighter in color. Transfer to a small bowl, add the celery, horseradish, mustard, green onion, parsley, Creole seasoning, celery salt, and paprika and blend thoroughly with a spatula. Store in an airtight container in the refrigerator for up to 7 days.

CHOW CHOW MAKES ABOUT 2 CUPS

2 ears fresh corn, shucked

¼ cup chopped pickled okra

2 tablespoons diced Roasted Red Bell Pepper (page 99)

¼ cup minced onion

1 tablespoon Creole mustard

1 tablespoon chopped Italian flat-leaf parsley leaves

2 tablespoons chopped green onion, green parts only

2 tablespoons Steen's cane vinegar

Preheat the oven to 400°F.

Place the corn on a baking sheet and roast for 8 minutes. Turn over the corn and roast for another 7 minutes, or until it begins to color. Allow to cool, then cut the corn kernels off the cobs into a medium bowl. Discard the corncobs or reserve for another use.

Add the okra, roasted red pepper, onion, mustard, parsley, green onion, and vinegar to the corn and blend thoroughly with a rubber spatula. Cover and refrigerate to allow the flavors to marry, for at least 8 hours.

SHRIMP CREOLE SERVES 6

2 tablespoons blended oil or vegetable oil

1 cup minced onion

½ cup minced celery

½ cup minced green bell pepper

1 tablespoon minced garlic

3 cups diced Creole tomatoes (substitute 28 ounces canned if fresh not available)

2 cups Shrimp Stock (page 210)

Creole seasoning

2 pounds (21- to 24-count) Gulf shrimp, peeled and deveined

½ cup (1 stick) unsalted butter, cut into cubes

Cooked long-grain white rice, for serving

Green onions, sliced, for serving

Warm the oil in a large Dutch oven set over medium heat. Add the onion, celery, and bell pepper and cook until the onion is translucent, about 10 minutes.

Add the garlic and cook until fragrant, about 1 minute. Add the tomatoes and cook until they start to break down, about 20 minutes.

Add the stock and the Creole seasoning and stir. Reduce the heat to medium-low and cook until the mixture is reduced by one third, about 30 minutes.

Add the shrimp and stir. Increase the heat to medium and simmer the shrimp in the sauce until they are firm and opaque, about 8 minutes. Remove the pan from the heat. Add in the butter, 1 cube at a time. Do not add more butter until each cube has melted. The sauce will thicken.

Serve the shrimp over rice and garnish with green onions.

SHRIMP AND GRITS SERVES 6

1 quart Shrimp Stock (page 210)

1 quart Veal Stock (page 212)

1 medium Roasted Red Bell Pepper (recipe follows), coarsely chopped

1½ pounds (21- to 25-count) Gulf shrimp, peeled and deveined

Creole seasoning

2 tablespoons blended oil or vegetable oil

2 tablespoons unsalted butter

Green onions, sliced, for serving

Stone-Ground Grits (page 178), for serving

Combine the stocks in a medium Dutch oven over medium-low heat and bring to a simmer. Cook until the liquid is reduced by one third, about 1½ hours.

Add the roasted bell pepper to the reduced stock and stir. Remove the pan from the heat.

Season the shrimp with Creole seasoning.

Warm the oil in a large cast-iron pan set over medium heat. When the oil shimmers, add the shrimp in a single layer and sear on one side until they turn pink and release easily from the pan, about 1 minute. Use tongs to turn the shrimp and sear the other side.

Ladle in 1 cup of the reduced stock sauce (you may have some sauce leftover). Reduce the heat to medium-low. Let the shrimp simmer in the stock until they are firm, pink, and opaque, about 2 minutes.

Remove the pan from the heat. Add the butter and stir with a wooden spoon until it melts. The sauce should be thick enough to coat the back of the wooden spoon.

Serve the shrimp and sauce over the grits and garnish with green onions.

ROASTED RED BELL PEPPER

1 medium red bell pepper

If you have a gas stove, turn the heat to high.

Using tongs with a heat-safe handle, hold the pepper directly atop the flame, turning every 30 seconds or so until the entire thing is black and blistered.

You can also put the pepper under the oven broiler and turn it every 2 minutes or so until it is blackened.

Put the blackened pepper in a bowl and cover with plastic wrap so the pepper will steam and cool. Once cool, slip the skin off the pepper under cool running water. Discard the skin, stem, and seeds.

FLAMBEAUX SHRIMP WITH MIRLITON SLAW SERVES 6

1 cup buttermilk

2 tablespoons hot sauce

1 pound (21- to 25-count) Gulf shrimp, peeled and deveined

Blended oil or vegetable oil, for frying

Seafood Dredge (page 213)

½ cup Crystal Honey Gastrique (recipe follows)

Mirliton Slaw with Caviar Ranch (page 63)

In a medium bowl, combine the buttermilk and the hot sauce and whisk. Add the shrimp and mix until well coated. Marinate in the refrigerator for 1 hour.

Heat the oil to 350°F in a deep fryer or Dutch oven. Line a plate with paper towels.

Pour the dredge in a large bowl. Add the shrimp and toss to coat. Shake off the excess.

Working in batches, if necessary, fry the shrimp in the hot oil until golden brown, 2 to 3 minutes. Drain the shrimp on the paper towel–lined plate.

In a large bowl, combine the hot shrimp with the gastrique and toss to coat. To serve, spoon the sauced shrimp over the slaw.

CRYSTAL HONEY GASTRIQUE MAKES 2 CUPS

1 cup Crystal hot sauce

1 cup local honey

2 tablespoons light brown sugar

Combine the hot sauce, honey, and brown sugar in a saucepan set over medium-low heat. Cook until the honey has melted and the mixture has thickened slightly, about 5 minutes.

OYSTERS ÉTOUFFÉE SERVES 6

2 quarts oysters, divided

1 cup blended oil or vegetable oil, plus more for frying

1 cup all-purpose flour

2 cups diced onions

1 cup diced celery

1 cup diced green bell pepper

1 tablespoon minced garlic

1 tablespoon tomato paste

2 bay leaves

Seafood Dredge (page 213)

2 egg whites

Stone-Ground Grits (page 178), for serving

Sliced green onions, for serving

Combine 1 quart of the oysters and their liquor in a food processor and pulse 4 or 5 times to break the oysters up a bit but not to liquefy, and set aside.

Pour the remaining 1 quart of oysters into a colander set over a bowl to catch the liquor. Do not discard the liquor. Set aside.

Make a dark roux. A large cast-iron Dutch oven is the best choice for making roux because of the way cast iron evenly retains heat. Use a roux spoon or a spoon with a flat end to constantly move and scrape the hot mixture around.

Start by warming the oil in the Dutch oven set over medium-high heat. Slowly add in the flour and start stirring. Stir constantly until the roux is a brick-red color, about 20 minutes.

Keep stirring while you add the onion, celery, and bell pepper. The roux will be hot. When it has turned into a thick, shiny mass, add the garlic, tomato paste, and bay leaves and give it a quick stir. Reduce the heat to medium. Stir in the reserved chopped oysters and cook for an additional 15 minutes.

Heat oil to 350°F in a deep fryer or Dutch oven. Line a plate with paper towels.

Pour the dredge into a large bowl. Pour the egg whites into a bowl and whisk until frothy. Add the oysters to the egg whites, mix until well coated, and let sit, refrigerated, for 15 minutes.

Strain the oysters from the egg whites. Add the oysters to the bowl with the dredge and toss to coat the oysters thoroughly. Shake off the excess dredge.

Working in batches, fry the oysters in the hot oil until golden brown, about 2 minutes. Drain the oysters on the paper towel–lined plate.

Remove the bay leaves and then serve the étouffée over the grits and top with green onions and the fried oysters.

OYSTER AND CAJUN CAVIAR PO' BOY SERVES 6

Blended oil or vegetable oil, for frying

Seafood Dredge (page 213)

2 egg whites

2 quarts oysters, drained

Caviar Ranch Dressing (page 204, see note), for serving

2 loaves French bread, cut into 6-inch lengths and then cut in half lengthwise

5 ounces fresh arugula, for serving

Set up a deep fryer or a large cast-iron Dutch oven with oil three-quarters of the way up the sides and heat to 350°F. Line a plate with paper towels.

Pour the dredge in a large bowl. Pour the egg whites into another bowl and whisk until frothy. Add the oysters to the egg whites and mix until well coated. Let sit, refrigerated, for 15 minutes.

Strain the oysters from the egg whites. Add the oysters to the bowl with the dredge and toss to coat the oysters thoroughly. Shake off the excess dredge.

Working in batches, fry the oysters in the hot oil until golden brown, about 2 minutes. Drain the oysters on the paper towel–lined plate.

Spread the Caviar Ranch on the French bread. Add oysters and top with fresh arugula.

OYSTER BLT SERVES 6

1 (8-ounce) slab pork belly, cut into 24 (2-inch-square, ½-inch-thick) pieces

Blended oil or vegetable oil, for frying

Seafood Dredge (page 213)

2 egg whites

1 quart oysters, drained

Tomato Jam (recipe follows), for serving

1 ounce micro arugula, for serving

In a 12-inch cast-iron skillet set over medium heat, cook the pork belly as you would bacon, 5 to 7 minutes per side. Set aside to drain on paper towels.

Heat the oil to 350°F in a deep fryer or Dutch oven. Line a plate with paper towels.

Pour the dredge into a large bowl. Pour the egg whites into a second bowl and whisk until frothy. Add the oysters to the egg whites and mix until well coated. Let sit, refrigerated, for 15 minutes.

Strain the oysters from the egg whites. Add the oysters to the bowl with the dredge and toss to coat the oysters evenly. Shake off the excess dredge. Working in batches, fry the oysters in the hot oil until golden brown, 2 to 3 minutes. Drain the oysters on the paper towel–lined plate.

To serve, spread some Tomato Jam on a small plate. Alternate 4 fried oysters and 4 pieces of pork belly over the jam. Top with micro arugula.

TOMATO JAM MAKES ABOUT 3 PINTS

2 pints cherry tomatoes

3 medium vine-ripened tomatoes, diced

½ cup Steen's cane vinegar

2 cups light Karo corn syrup

2 teaspoons kosher salt

1 tablespoon black pepper

Combine the tomatoes, vinegar, syrup, salt, and pepper in a saucepan set over low heat. Cook until the mixture has fully broken down, reduced by one third, and has a jam-like consistency. Store in the refrigerator for up to 14 days.

STUFFED DEVILED CRABS SERVES 6

Deviled crabs or devil crabs have Cuban origins and derive from south Florida. The original version is known to be hotter than hell. This recipe is not a spicy version, but you can add your own personal level of heat. Stuffed crabs have been in my family for generations. The dish is just another example of the broad influences of so many cultures that have thrown their hat into the ring, or melting pot, of New Orleans food and culture.

6 large whole boiled crabs

6 slices smoked bacon, chopped

2 teaspoons blended oil or vegetable oil

4 tablespoons, plus 6 thin pats unsalted butter

½ cup peeled, finely diced mirliton

½ cup diced onion

¼ cup diced celery

¼ cup diced green bell pepper

1 teaspoon minced garlic

½ cup Seafood Dredge (page 213)

¼ cup chopped green onions

2 tablespoons minced Italian flat-leaf parsley

¼ cup minced raw shrimp

¼ cup claw crabmeat, picked through for shells and cartilage

½ cup unseasoned breadcrumbs

Creole seasoning

Salad mix (optional)

Pick the crabmeat from the shells and set aside.

Wash and thoroughly dry each of the top crab shells. Set aside. Discard the rest of the shells or reserve them for stock.

Preheat the oven to 350°F.

Combine the bacon and oil in a skillet over medium heat and cook until the fat has rendered out and the bacon is brick-red, about 10 minutes.

Add 4 tablespoons of the butter and let it melt. Add the mirliton, onion, celery, and bell pepper and cook, stirring occasionally, until the vegetables soften, about 10 minutes. Add the garlic and cook until fragrant, about 1 minute.

Add the stock, green onions, and parsley. Reduce the temperature to low and simmer until the liquid is slightly reduced and tinted green in color, about 20 minutes. The mirliton should be almost soft.

Add the shrimp and cook, stirring frequently, until the shrimp is fully pink, about 4 minutes. Remove the skillet from the heat. Add the reserved crabmeat and the claw meat. Using a rubber spatula to stir very gently, add the breadcrumbs, a little at a time, to achieve a stuffing consistency. Season with Creole seasoning.

Mound the stuffing into the reserved crab shells. Put them in a large baking dish or rimmed baking sheet. Dot the top of each crab with 1 pat of butter. Cover tightly with aluminum foil and bake for 30 minutes.

Remove the foil and bake until the top of the stuffing is golden, about 5 minutes. Take care to not overcook and scorch the tips of shells. Serve hot individually or on top of your favorite salad mix for a great starter to any meal.

FRIED SOFT-SHELL CRAB ON SUMMER TOMATO SALAD SERVES 4

Soft-shell crabs are the ultimate treat. Once you have cleaned them you can eat the whole thing, shell and all, because the crabs have recently molted their old exoskeleton and are still soft. There is a very brief window of time in which you can harvest these crabs before their shells harden again. Keep them stored in the refrigerator on a damp paper towel on a plate with another damp paper towel over the crabs so they don't dry out.

Blended oil or vegetable oil, for frying

8 cups all-purpose flour

2 tablespoons Creole seasoning

2 large eggs

2 cups whole milk

8 cups unseasoned breadcrumbs

4 jumbo soft-shell Gulf crabs, cleaned

1 (4-ounce) bag mixed salad greens

1 pint mixed heirloom cherry tomatoes, halved

6 tablespoons Citrus Vinaigrette (page 206)

1 pound jumbo lump crabmeat, picked over for shells and cartilage

Preheat the oven to its lowest temperature. Line a platter with paper towels.

Set up a deep fryer or a large cast-iron Dutch oven three-quarters of the way up the sides with the oil and heat to 350°F.

In a medium bowl, mix together the flour and Creole seasoning. In another medium bowl, mix together the eggs and milk to make an egg wash. Pour the breadcrumbs onto a large plate.

Coat each soft-shell crab thoroughly in flour, then dip in egg wash, then breadcrumbs. Set them on a platter, making sure they are not touching.

When the oil comes to temperature, lift each crab around the center of its body with a pair of tongs. The shell should face up and the legs should be hanging down. Slowly lower the legs into the oil first and hold them there for 15 seconds to crisp up, then carefully lower the crab into the oil. Use caution when submerging the crabs in the oil. They may pop and release water as they cook. When the crabs first hit the oil, they will be very "noisy" as the liquid escapes from them and vaporizes. Listen carefully—when they start to quiet down, they are close to being done. They are ready when they are fully golden brown, 3 to 5 minutes. Using tongs, grasp the center of the crab with the legs hanging and lift it from the oil.

Drain the crab on the paper towel–lined platter and put it in the oven to keep warm while you fry the rest.

Toss the salad greens, tomatoes, and vinaigrette in a bowl. Add the jumbo lump crabmeat, and gently toss again, taking care to keep the lumps intact.

Serve each crab belly-side up. Top with the tomato salad.

WHOLE FRIED SPECKLED TROUT ALMONDINE SERVES 4

Amandine, sometimes Anglicized as almondine, is a culinary term indicating a garnish of toasted almonds. In New Orleans, the great haute Creole restaurants have all indulged in this simple preparation of a classic French favorite. The use of browned butter and warm toasted almonds will leave a lasting memory for your family and friends for a long time. We like to use speckled trout or spotted sea trout for this dish, but you can substitute with your favorite local catch. The magic is in the sauce.

2 cups sliced almonds

Blended oil or vegetable oil, for frying

2 whole speckled trout, gilled, gutted, scaled, and scored

4 cups cornstarch

2 tablespoons Creole seasoning

Meunière Sauce (recipe follows), for serving

Preheat the oven to 300°F. Line a platter with paper towels.

Put the almonds in a baking dish or roasting pan and bake, stirring every 5 minutes or so, just until they begin to take on color, 10 to 15 minutes. They will continue to darken as they cool. Set aside.

Add enough oil to come halfway up the sides of a stainless-steel pot large enough to accommodate the whole fish.

In a bowl, mix together the cornstarch and Creole seasoning. Dredge the fish in the seasoned cornstarch.

Submerge the fish in the hot oil. Cook until golden brown with an internal temperature of 145°F, 8 to 10 minutes. Use a wooden spoon to press the flesh of the fish. It should be firm to the touch with no give.

Remove the fish from the oil using two pairs of kitchen tongs, one positioned just below the head, another positioned just in front of the tail. Allow the oil to drain off into the pot for a moment. Drain the fish on the paper towel–lined platter.

To serve, put the whole fish on a platter and top with the toasted almonds and Meunière Sauce.

MEUNIÈRE SAUCE MAKES 3 CUPS

1 cup (2 sticks) unsalted butter

1 cup Worcestershire sauce

1 cup fresh lemon juice

1 tablespoon minced Italian flat-leaf parsley

Melt the butter in a medium saucepan over low heat. The color will change from bright yellow to golden tan then quickly to deep golden brown. When it smells toasty, is deep-golden brown, and browned milk solids appear in the bottom of the pan, take the pan off the heat.

Whisking constantly, add the Worcestershire sauce and lemon juice. The sauce will froth. When it stops frothing, stir in the parsley. The sauce can be refrigerated for 7 days.

BAKED FLOUNDER WITH SHRIMP AND MIRLITON DRESSING SERVES 4 TO 6

2 tablespoons unsalted butter, softened

2 whole flounders, scaled and butterflied for stuffing

Creole seasoning

Shrimp and Mirliton Dressing (page 182)

Lemon halves, for serving

Preheat the oven to 400°F.Grease two baking sheets with the softened butter.

Season the flounders, inside and out, with the Creole seasoning. Center each flounder on one of the baking sheets. Working from the center of each fish, open the fillets to either side like a book. Stuff the dressing into the cavities of each fish. Fold the fillets back over the dressing.

Bake for 8 minutes, or until the fillets have rolled back to show the dressing, which should be lightly browned. The skin will be crisp. The fillets should be firm, opaque, and flake easily with a fork. Rotate the baking pans if your oven will not accommodate them on one rack.

Serve the flounder with the lemon halves.

REDFISH ON THE HALF SHELL SERVES 6

3 to 4 pounds whole redfish, gilled and gutted with skin and scales left intact

Creole seasoning

3 tablespoons unsalted butter

3 whole lemons, cut in half, for serving

Preheat the oven to 400°F.

Cut each fish in half. Season the fish liberally with Creole seasoning.

Melt 1½ tablespoons of the butter in a 12-inch cast-iron skillet set over medium-high heat. Working in batches and using the remaining butter as needed, add the fish, flesh-side down, and the lemons, cut sides down, and sear for 2 minutes. When the fish releases easily from the pan, turn it with a fish spatula and sear it, skin-side down, for 2 minutes. Transfer the fish to one or two large, rimmed baking sheets.

Remove the lemons and set aside.

Bake for 6 minutes, or until the fish is firm, opaque, and flakes easily with a fork. Serve with the charred lemons.

<< Baked Flounder with Shrimp and Mirliton Dressing

WHOLE REDFISH COURT-BOUILLON SERVES 4 TO 6

1 (18- to 20-inch) redfish (3 to 4 pounds), cleaned, gutted, and scales removed

4 lemons, halved and charred under a broiler, plus more for serving

1 tablespoon kosher salt, plus more as needed

1 tablespoon black pepper, plus more as needed

1 tablespoon Creole seasoning, plus more as needed

8 Creole tomatoes or other beefy vine-ripened tomatoes

1 cup blended oil or vegetable oil

¾ cup chopped celery

1¼ cups chopped white onions

2 green bell peppers, chopped

1 tablespoon chopped garlic

Leaves from 1 bunch Italian flat-leaf parsley, chopped, plus more for garnish

½ cup all-purpose flour

¼ cup tomato paste

4 cups Shrimp Stock (page 210)

1 blue crab, cleaned, halved

Cooked long-grain white rice, for serving

In a large bowl, prepare an ice bath with half ice and half water.

Use a small sharp knife to score the fish along both sides all the way to the spine.

Squeeze lemon juice over both sides of the fish. Reserve the lemon hulls. Season the fish inside and out with the salt, pepper, and Creole seasoning. Put the fish on a baking sheet and refrigerate.

In a medium stockpot over medium-high heat, bring 8 cups of water to a boil. Using a paring knife, make small X marks in the bottoms of the tomatoes, and put them in the boiling water. Cook the tomatoes until the skin starts to curl back around the cuts, 3 to 4 minutes. Transfer the tomatoes to the ice bath and let stand until cool. Peel the tomatoes and discard the skin. Coarsely chop the tomatoes and set aside.

Heat the oil in a large cast-iron Dutch oven over medium-high heat until the oil shimmers. Add the celery, onions, and bell peppers and cook, stirring frequently, until the onions are translucent, about 8 minutes. Add the garlic and parsley and cook, stirring, until the garlic is fragrant, about 1 minute.

Sift the flour into the Dutch oven while stirring with a wooden spoon. Add the tomato paste, mix well, and cook, stirring often, until caramelized, about 4 minutes.

Preheat the oven to 350°F.

Slowly add the stock, crab, and reserved tomatoes to the pot and cook, stirring often, until it comes to a simmer. Reduce the heat to low and add the reserved lemon hulls. Taste and season with salt, pepper, and Creole seasoning. Simmer, stirring occasionally, until the sauce is thick enough to coat the back of a spoon, about 40 minutes. Keep the sauce warm.

Bake the redfish for 45 minutes, or until the flesh is firm, opaque, and flakes easily with a fork.

To serve, ladle the tomato sauce onto a deep-sided platter. Add the fish and crab. Garnish with lemon and parsley. Serve with rice.

SEARED GROUPER WITH SATSUMA BEURRE BLANC SERVES 6

6 (6-ounce) skinless grouper fillets

Creole seasoning

4 tablespoons blended oil or vegetable oil

1 cup (2 sticks) unsalted butter, half cut into cubes

3 tablespoons minced shallot

3 tablespoons Steen's cane vinegar

1 medium satsuma (can substitute a clementine or blood orange), peeled and segmented

3 tablespoons dry white wine

½ cup heavy cream

Kosher salt

Black pepper

3 lemons, cut into wedges, for serving

Preheat the oven to 375°F.

Season the fish with Creole seasoning. Working in batches, if necessary, warm 2 tablespoons of oil in a 12-inch cast iron skillet over medium-high heat. Sear the fish on both sides then transfer to a rimmed baking sheet while you sear the rest of the fish, using the remaining oil as needed.

Bake the fillets for 4 to 5 minutes, or until the fish is firm, opaque, and flakes easily with a fork.

To make the sauce, melt 1 stick of butter in a small saucepan set over medium heat. Put the remaining butter cubes in the refrigerator.

Add the shallot to the saucepan and cook until translucent, about 2 minutes. Add the vinegar, satsuma, and wine and cook, stirring often, until the liquid is reduced by half, about 6 minutes.

Add the heavy cream, season with salt and pepper, and cook until the sauce is thick enough to coat the back of a spoon, about 6 minutes.

Pass the sauce through a fine-mesh strainer or chinois, pressing on the solids to extract as much liquid as possible. Discard the solids and add the sauce back to the saucepan over low heat. Whisk in the remaining butter, 1 cube at a time, until all butter has been incorporated. Add salt if needed.

To serve, using a large spoon, ladle some finished sauce onto each plate. Place the fish in the center of the plate. Garnish with lemon wedges.

CATFISH AMANDINE SERVES 6

2 cups buttermilk

½ cup hot sauce

6 (6-ounce) catfish fillets

1 cup (2 sticks) unsalted butter

½ cup Worcestershire sauce

½ cup fresh lemon juice

1 tablespoon chopped curly parsley

Blended oil or vegetable oil, for frying

Seafood Dredge (page 213)

Smothered Green Beans (page 168), for serving

1½ cups toasted sliced almonds, for serving

Combine the buttermilk and the hot sauce in a large bowl. Add the catfish and turn to coat. Cover, and marinate for 30 minutes in the refrigerator.

To make the sauce, heat a heavy-bottom saucepan over medium heat. Add the butter and whisk as it melts. Once melted, the butter will foam up. Stop cooking when the butter is an amber color and smells nutty, 8 to 10 minutes.

Add the Worcestershire sauce and the lemon juice. The butter will react fiercely to the acids, then settle down. Bring the mixture to a boil. Add the parsley and allow it to fry for a moment in the hot sauce. Set the pan aside in a warm place.

Preheat the oven to the lowest possible setting.

Add enough oil to reach halfway up the sides of a deep fryer or 12-inch cast-iron skillet, and heat the oil to 350°F. Line a plate with paper towels.

Pour the dredge into a shallow baking dish. Drain the catfish in a colander and discard the marinade. Thoroughly coat each piece of fish with the dredge.

Working in batches, fry each fish fillet until it is golden brown and firm to the touch, 5 to 7 minutes. Drain on the paper towel–lined plate and keep warm in the oven while you finish frying the rest of the fish.

Serve the fish over the green beans. Top the fish with the toasted almonds, then the sauce.

CAST-IRON SWORDFISH WITH SAUTÉED SUMMER VEGETABLES SERVES 6

6 (6-ounce) local swordfish fillets

Creole seasoning

2 large zucchini

2 large yellow squash

8 tablespoons unsalted butter, divided

1½ teaspoons minced garlic

2 pints cherry tomatoes, halved

3 lemons, halved, for serving

Season the fish on both sides with Creole seasoning. Set aside.

Cut the zucchini and the squash in half lengthwise, then cut into half-moons.

Melt 4 tablespoons of butter in a 12-inch cast-iron skillet set over medium-high heat. Add the zucchini and the yellow squash and cook until the edges of the vegetables begin to brown, about 4 minutes. Add the garlic and tomatoes and cook until fragrant, about 1 minute. Season with Creole seasoning. Remove the pan from the heat and hold the vegetables in the pan to keep warm.

Heat another cast-iron pan to medium-high heat and add 2 tablespoons unsalted butter. When the butter has melted and is sizzling, add the swordfish fillets. Cook, undisturbed, until the fish is seared and golden underneath, about 4 minutes. Carefully turn the fish with a fish spatula. Add the remaining 2 tablespoons of butter. Cook the fish for an additional 3 minutes. Tilting the pan toward you, use a tablespoon to repeatedly spoon the melted butter over the fish. The fish is cooked when the center of the fish feels firm to the touch.

With a large spoon, place the vegetable mixture in the center of the plate. With a spatula, place the fish on top of the vegetables. Spoon the remaining butter on top of the dish. Serve with halved lemons.

SEARED BLACK DRUM
WITH SAUTÉED CRABMEAT SERVES 6

¾ cup (1½ sticks) unsalted butter, divided

1 pound jumbo lump crabmeat, picked over for shells and cartilage

6 (6- to 7-ounce) fillets red or black drum

Creole seasoning

6 small lemon wedges

Minced Italian flat-leaf parsley, for garnish

Melt 1 stick of butter in a small saucepan over low heat. Add the crabmeat and stir very carefully to avoid breaking up those delicate lumps. Heat the crabmeat until just warmed through. Set aside and keep warm.

Season the fish generously on both sides with Creole seasoning.

Preheat the oven to the lowest possible setting.

Melt the remaining butter in a 12-inch cast-iron skillet over medium heat. Add the fish fillets in a single layer with space between them and cook until seared and golden, 2 to 3 minutes. Use a fish spatula to carefully turn the fish and sear the other side. The edges of the fish will be firm, opaque, and flake easily with a fork when done. If you are working in batches, set the first batch of fish on a plate in the oven while you sear the rest of the fish.

To serve, place a fillet on each plate. Spoon the crabmeat over the fish. Squeeze a lemon wedge over each portion, and garnish with parsley.

MEAT AND GAME

Just as our waterways and bayous are plentiful with fine seafood, our marshes, rice fields, and woodlands are home to an abundance of wild game. And our farmers produce some of the best beef and pork on the market. Weekend hunting trips with friends and family and enjoying the outdoors are some of the many fond memories I have of growing up. Sharing meals of wild rabbit fricassee, duck and andouille gumbo, and venison seared in cast iron over an open fire brings back memories and tales of the hunt.

BRAISED LAMB SHANKS WITH STONE-GROUND GRITS SERVES 6

Before you get started, read the recipe. The lamb must marinate overnight, roast, then braise for hours. It is not quick, but it is easy, worth the time, and the flavors are boldly aromatic and will fill your kitchen with herbal aromas, especially on a cold day.

FOR THE MARINADE

Leaves from 1 bunch Italian flat-leaf parsley, chopped

¼ cup diced green onions

1 tablespoon minced garlic

1 medium jalapeño (remove the seeds and membrane for less heat), minced

1 tablespoon Worcestershire sauce

1 medium onion, coarsely chopped

1 tablespoon kosher salt

1 teaspoon black pepper

FOR THE LAMB

6 lamb shanks

1 (28-ounce) can crushed tomatoes

2 tablespoons tomato paste

2 cups Beef Stock (page 211)

2 tablespoons blended oil or vegetable oil

2 cups diced onions

1 cup diced celery

1 cup diced green bell pepper

1 cup hearty red wine

1 tablespoon Creole mustard

Stone-Ground Grits (page 178), for serving

MARINADE

Combine the parsley, green onions, garlic, jalapeño, Worcestershire sauce, onion, salt, and pepper in a bowl and mix well.

LAMB

Rub the lamb shanks thoroughly with the marinade. Transfer the lamb to a container, pour the remaining marinade over it, seal, and refrigerate overnight.

Preheat the oven to 400°F.

Remove the lamb from the marinade and place it in a baking dish. Set the marinade aside. Roast, turning halfway through, for 45 minutes. Set the lamb aside while you make the braising liquid.

Reduce the oven heat to 350°F.

Combine the crushed tomatoes, tomato paste, and stock in a food processor and process until smooth. Set aside.

Heat the oil in a medium saucepan set over medium-high heat. Add the onions, celery, and bell pepper and cook the vegetables until they have softened, about 15 minutes.

Add the red wine. Use a wooden spoon to scrape the brown bits from the bottom of the pan. Add the reserved marinade and the reserved tomato and broth mixture and stir. Reduce the heat to low and simmer until the liquid has reduced by half, about 15 minutes.

Pour the reduced braising liquid over the lamb shanks. Cover the pan with aluminum foil and bake for 2½ hours. The meat should be very tender and fall from the bones.

Serve with Stone-Ground Grits.

RACK OF LAMB PERSILLADE WITH JOLLOF RICE SERVES 6

Persillade in its simplest form is no more than parsley chopped with garlic. Using curry powder instead of garlic adds an aromatic and complex flavor to this simple preparation. Recipes like this are just an example of how regional availability and resourceful cooks can create unique and memorable dishes that are shared with friends and family. Having the ability to source a variety of ingredients and mix in different cultural influences is the origins of Creole cuisine and the recipe for a great dining experience.

3 (8-bone) racks of lamb

Kosher salt

Black pepper

2 tablespoons blended oil or vegetable oil

1 quart unseasoned breadcrumbs

Leaves from 1 bunch curly parsley

1 tablespoon Curry Powder (recipe follows)

¾ cup Dijon mustard

Jollof Rice (recipe follows), for serving

Cut each rack of lamb into 2 (4-bone) chops and season with salt and pepper.

Heat the oil in a 12-inch cast-iron skillet over medium heat. When the oil shimmers, and working in batches, give the chops a hard sear on both sides, 1½ to 2 minutes per side. They will still be very rare. Transfer the chops to a rack. Set the rack in the refrigerator for a minimum of 1 hour to thoroughly chill the lamb.

Preheat the oven to 350°F.

Make the breading for the chops. Combine the breadcrumbs and parsley in a food processor and pulse until mixed. Add the curry powder and pulse to make a persillade. Transfer the persillade to a large bowl.

Transfer the lamb chops from the refrigerator to a baking sheet in one layer, making sure they don't touch. Coat the chops with the mustard, taking care to avoid the bones. Cover the mustard with the persillade breading.

Bake until the chops reach an internal temperature of 135°F for medium-rare. Allow the chops to rest for 4 minutes.

Cut each 4-bone rack into individual chops. Serve with Jollof Rice.

continued >>

JOLLOF RICE SERVES 6

2 medium Roma tomatoes, chopped

1 (14.5-ounce) can diced tomatoes with juices

1 tablespoon tomato paste

1 red bell pepper, seeded and diced

½ medium red onion, coarsely chopped

½ teaspoon dried thyme

1 teaspoon smoked paprika

½ teaspoon ground cayenne pepper

1 teaspoon Curry Powder (recipe follows)

¼ cup blended oil or vegetable oil

1 tablespoon unsalted butter

1 cup basmati rice

2 cups hot water

1 teaspoon kosher salt, plus more as needed

2 bay leaves

Black pepper

In a blender, combine the Roma tomatoes, diced tomatoes, tomato paste, bell pepper, onion, thyme, smoked paprika, cayenne, and curry powder and purée until smooth.

Transfer the mixture to a medium cast-iron Dutch oven set over medium heat and bring to a simmer. Reduce the heat to low and simmer, uncovered, until the mixture is reduced to a tight paste, 15 to 20 minutes.

Increase the heat to medium-high. Add the oil and butter and stir until the butter melts. Add the rice and stir until the rice is toasted, looks opaque, and smells toasted, 5 to 7 minutes.

Add the hot water, the salt, and bay leaves, stir well, and bring to a boil. Cover tightly, then reduce the heat to the lowest setting and cook for 10 minutes.

Remove from the heat, fluff the rice, cover again, and let the rice steam off the heat for 10 minutes more. Season with salt and pepper, as needed.

CURRY POWDER MAKES ¾ CUP

1½ teaspoons ground turmeric

1 tablespoon ground coriander seeds

1 tablespoon whole cumin seeds

2 tablespoons allspice

2 tablespoons ground ginger

2 tablespoons yellow mustard seeds

2 tablespoons ground fenugreek seeds

1½ teaspoons ground black pepper

1 whole clove or ¼ teaspoon ground

Combine the turmeric, coriander seeds, cumin seeds, allspice, ginger, mustard seeds, fenugreek seeds, pepper, and clove in a spice grinder and grind, or crush with a mortar and pestle.

Store in a sealed jar.

SMOTHERED QUAIL SERVES 6

12 dressed domestic or wild bone-in skinless quail

Creole seasoning

2 tablespoons blended oil or vegetable oil

1 large white onion, julienned

1 cup Chicken Stock (page 209)

Cooked long-grain white rice, for serving

Season the quail with Creole seasoning.

Heat the oil in a 12-inch cast-iron skillet set over medium-high heat. When the oil shimmers, add the quail, breast-side down, and cook until the quail are hard seared and release easily from the pan, about 10 minutes. Transfer the quail to a plate.

Preheat the oven to 350ºF.

Add the onion to the skillet, and cook over medium-high heat until it has begun to caramelize, about 8 minutes. Add the stock and deglaze the pan, using a wooden spoon to scrape up the brown bits. Reduce the heat to medium and simmer until the liquid has reduced by one third, about 10 minutes.

Return the quail to the pan, breast-side up. Slide the pan into the oven and bake until the quail has an internal temperature of 165ºF, about 15 minutes.

Serve with rice and top with sauce from the pan.

WHOLE ROASTED DUCK
WITH SUGARCANE GLAZE SERVES 6

1 (3-pound) wild or domestic duck, cleaned, rinsed, and patted dry

Kosher salt

Black pepper

2 tablespoons blended oil or vegetable oil

¼ cup Steen's cane syrup

Preheat the oven to 350°F.

Season the duck liberally inside and out with salt and pepper.

Heat the oil in a 12-inch cast-iron skillet set over medium heat. Place the duck in the pan, skin-side down, and sear until the skin is crispy, 4 to 5 minutes. Turn the duck skin-side up, place the skillet in the oven, and roast for 15 minutes.

Remove the skillet from the oven. Use a pastry brush or spoon to apply half the cane syrup evenly over the exterior of the duck. Return the skillet to the oven and bake until the interior reaches 130°F at the breastbone for medium-rare, about 10 minutes. Baste the duck again with the remaining cane syrup. The skin will be deeply burnished and crisp. Rest the duck for 5 minutes before serving.

SEARED VENISON BACKSTRAP SERVES 6

2 (1¼- to 1½-pound) whole venison backstraps, silver skins removed

Kosher salt

Black pepper

1 tablespoon blended oil or vegetable oil

1 tablespoon unsalted butter

1 (12-ounce) bottle beer of choice

2 sprigs fresh rosemary

Season the venison with salt and pepper. Set aside.

Place a 12-inch cast-iron skillet over medium-high heat for 2 minutes. Add the oil and heat until shimmering. Working in batches, if necessary, add the backstraps to the pan and give them a hard sear on all sides, about 2 minutes per side.

Add the butter, beer, and rosemary and cook to an internal temperature of 135°F for medium rare. Carefully tilt the pan every couple of minutes so the sauce gathers in one area of the pan so you can spoon the sauce over the meat.

Transfer the venison from the sauce to a plate and set aside to rest for 5 minutes. Return the skillet to the heat and cook until the sauce has reduced by half, about 5 minutes. Remove and discard the rosemary. Slice the meat and serve with the pan sauce.

GLAZED SMOKED HOLIDAY HAM SERVES 10 TO 12

1 (8- to 10-pound) smoked spiral-cut ham

7 garlic cloves, peeled

2 (3-inch) sprigs fresh rosemary

3 cups root beer (not sugar-free), preferably Barq's

1 cup dark brown sugar

½ cup (1 stick) unsalted butter, cut into cubes

Preheat the oven to 400°F.

Place the ham in a roasting pan, cut-side down, so the bone is sticking up. Scatter the garlic cloves and the rosemary springs around the pan.

Pour the root beer over the ham, ensuring that some of it runs down into the spiral cuts.

Pat the brown sugar over the ham with your hands so it sticks and gets into the spiral cuts. Cover the ham with aluminum foil and bake for 45 minutes.

Remove the foil and return the ham to the oven until the brown sugar has caramelized, about 15 minutes.

Remove the ham from the oven and baste it with the pan juices. Let the ham rest for 20 minutes, basting every 4 to 5 minutes.

Save the leftover bone to season a pot of beans.

OSSO BUCCO EN BIANCO
WITH MASCARPONE POLENTA SERVES 6

1 bunch Italian flat-leaf parsley, leaves only, finely minced

1 small carrot, peeled and finely diced

2 garlic cloves, very finely minced

Zest of 1 lemon

6 (1-pound) bone-in veal shanks

Kosher salt

Black pepper

2 tablespoons blended oil or vegetable oil

1 large red onion, coarsely chopped

2 large carrots, peeled and coarsely chopped

2 whole heads garlic, unpeeled and cut in half crosswise

2 (6-inch) sprigs fresh rosemary

2 bay leaves

1 (750-ml) bottle dry white wine

1 quart Beef Stock (page 211)

Mascarpone Polenta (page 178), for serving

In a small bowl, combine the parsley, diced carrot, minced garlic, and lemon zest and mix well to make a gremolata. Cover and set aside.

Preheat the oven to 350°F.

Season the veal shanks with salt and pepper.

Heat the oil in a large Dutch oven set over medium-high heat. When the oil shimmers add the veal shanks and sear on all sides until golden brown, about 3 minutes per side, turning with tongs as you go. Transfer the shanks to a plate.

Add the onion and chopped carrot to the pot and cook, stirring often, until caramelized, about 7 minutes.

Add the garlic heads, rosemary, bay leaves, and wine, stir, and cook until reduced by half, about 20 minutes.

Add the stock and return the veal shanks to the pot. Cover and bake in the oven for about 1½ hours, or until the meat is fork tender and pulling away from the bones.

Gently remove the meat from the sauce and arrange on a platter. Strain the sauce into a bowl and discard the solids. Serve the osso bucco with polenta, sauce, and the reserved gremolata.

RABBIT FRICASSEE SERVES 6

1 (3-pound) rabbit, skinned, cleaned, and quartered

Kosher salt

Black pepper

2 tablespoons blended oil or vegetable oil

1 cup diced onion

½ cup diced green bell pepper

½ cup diced celery

1 tablespoon tomato paste

½ cup hearty red wine

1 whole head garlic, unpeeled, cut in half lengthwise

Cooked long-grain white rice, for serving

Season the rabbit generously with salt and pepper. Set the tenderloin aside.

Heat the oil in a 12-inch cast-iron skillet set over medium-high heat. When the oil shimmers, add the rabbit pieces, except the tenderloin, to the hot pan. Give the rabbit a hard sear on all sides, turning as necessary, 3 to 4 minutes per side. Set the rabbit pieces aside.

Add the tenderloin to the pan and give it a hard sear on all sides, turning as necessary. Transfer the tenderloin to the plate with the rabbit pieces.

Add the onion, bell pepper, and celery to the hot pan and cook, stirring frequently, until the vegetables begin to caramelize, about 8 minutes.

Add the tomato paste, stir thoroughly, and cook for 4 minutes.

Add the wine and deglaze the pan, using a wooden spoon to scrape the brown bits from the bottom. Cook until reduced by half, about 8 minutes.

Add the garlic and the reserved rabbit, reduce the heat to low, cover, and simmer, stirring occasionally to avoid sticking, for 45 minutes. The rabbit is done when the meat is pulling away from the bone.

Serve with white rice.

PAN-FRIED FROG LEGS WITH GARLIC BUTTER SERVES 6

2 cups all-purpose flour

Kosher salt

Black pepper

18 frog legs, cleaned

Blended oil or vegetable oil

Garlic Butter (recipe follows)

French bread, for serving

Preheat the oven to 350°F. Lightly oil a baking sheet.

Combine the flour, salt, and pepper in a bowl and mix well. Lightly dust the frog legs with the seasoned flour. Set aside.

Working in batches, heat 1 tablespoon of oil in a 12-inch cast-iron skillet set over medium heat. When the oil shimmers, add the frog legs in a single layer, so they are not touching. Sear the frog legs until a rich caramel color develops, about 2 minutes per side. Transfer them to a plate. Repeat with additional oil and the remaining frog legs.

Do not wash or wipe out the skillet. Just set it aside.

Arrange the seared frog legs in a single layer on the prepared baking sheet. Bake for 10 minutes.

While the frog legs are finishing in the oven, return the skillet to low heat. Add the Garlic Butter to the skillet and use a wooden spoon to scrape the brown bits from the pan. Continue stirring until the butter is melted.

Place the frog legs on a platter and spoon the sauce over them. Serve with hot French bread.

GARLIC BUTTER MAKES ABOUT ¾ CUP

1 cup (2 sticks) unsalted butter, softened

2 tablespoons chopped garlic

2 tablespoons chopped green onion

Leaves from ½ bunch Italian flat-leaf parsley, chopped

1 teaspoon Creole seasoning

¼ teaspoon paprika

Use an electric mixer to whip the butter until it is aerated and slightly lighter in color.

Transfer the butter to a small bowl, add the garlic, green onion, parsley, Creole seasoning, and paprika and blend thoroughly with a spatula.

Store in an airtight container in the refrigerator for up to 7 days.

CREOLE SHORT RIB DAUBE SERVES 6

4 pounds boneless beef short ribs (have your butcher cut them into 10-ounce portions)

Creole seasoning

2 tablespoons blended oil or vegetable oil

1 medium onion, quartered

4 stalks celery, chopped

1 medium carrot, peeled and diced

2 tablespoons tomato paste

½ cup peeled garlic cloves

1 cup red wine

2 cups Beef Stock (page 211)

Mashed potatoes, for serving

Season the short ribs with Creole seasoning. Set aside.

Set a large cast-iron Dutch oven over medium-high heat. Add the oil and heat until shimmering. Working in batches, if necessary, add the ribs and give them a hard sear on both sides. Set aside.

Add the onion, celery, and carrot and cook until the vegetables soften and begin to caramelize, about 8 minutes.

Add the tomato paste, stir thoroughly, and cook until caramelized, about 4 minutes. Add the garlic and cook until fragrant, about 1 minute. Add the wine and deglaze the pan using a wooden spoon to scrape up the brown bits. Cook until it has reduced by a third, about 6 minutes.

Return the seared ribs to the pot. Add enough stock to cover. Place a lid on top, reduce the heat to low, and simmer until fork-tender, about 90 minutes.

Serve on top of mashed potatoes, topped with liquid from the pot.

CAST-IRON PORK TENDERLOIN WITH BLUEBERRY JUS SERVES 6

1 (3-pound) boneless pork tenderloin

Creole seasoning

2 tablespoons blended oil or vegetable oil

½ pint fresh blueberries

½ cup hot water

Smothered Potatoes (page 163), for serving

Preheat the oven to 350°F.

Season the pork generously with the Creole seasoning.

Heat the oil in a cast-iron Dutch oven set over medium-high heat. Add the pork and give it an all-around hard sear, turning with tongs as you go. The exterior of the pork should be a deep golden brown, 4 to 5 minutes per side.

Place the pork in a roasting pan, place in the oven, and cook until the pork reaches an internal temperature of 145°F.

Remove the pork from the pan and let rest, uncovered, for 5 minutes.

While the pork is resting, make the blueberry jus. Set the roasting pan on the stove over medium-high heat. Add the blueberries and hot water and cook, using a wooden spoon to scrape up the browned bits on the bottom of the pan. Reduce the liquid by half, about 5 minutes.

Cut the pork into 1-inch slices and fan them out on a platter. Spoon the sauce over the pork. Serve with Smothered Potatoes.

POULTRY

Poultry is the most versatile ingredient available to the Creole cook. From classic preparations such as Chicken Clemenceau to the basic poultry stock, its availability and versatility are almost endless. Using the simple ingredients and techniques in these recipes can transform the everyday meal into the piece de resistance of any family gathering. Simplicity is at the heart of every Creole recipe in its origins, and the preparations in this chapter can be used as a guide to deepen your curiosity to explore the many storied offerings that have shaped the evolution of some of the finest menus in Louisiana.

WHOLE ROASTED CHICKEN WITH ROOT VEGETABLES AND PAN GRAVY SERVES 6

1 (3-pound) whole chicken

Creole seasoning for seasoning, plus 2 tablespoons

3 tablespoons blended oil or vegetable oil, divided

2 pounds red and/or Yukon Gold potatoes, unpeeled and quartered

1 whole head garlic, halved crosswise

3 carrots, peeled and halved

4 sprigs fresh thyme

1 cup Chicken Stock (page 209)

Kosher salt

Black pepper

Preheat the oven to 325°F.

If the neck and a gizzard packet is inside the chicken, remove it and discard. Rinse the chicken inside and out with water and dry with paper towels. Season the chicken inside and out with the Creole seasoning.

Heat 2 tablespoons of the oil in a 14-inch cast-iron skillet set over medium-high heat. Add the chicken and sear for 3 minutes per side, using tongs to turn as you go. Transfer the chicken to a plate. Do not wipe out or wash the pan.

To the hot pan, add the potatoes, garlic, carrots, the remaining 1 tablespoon of oil, the 2 tablespoons of Creole seasoning, and the thyme.

Return the skillet to the heat. Add the stock and deglaze the pan by using a wooden spoon to scrape the browned bits from the bottom. This is the beginning of your pan gravy.

Add the chicken back to the center of the pan on top of the vegetables.

Place the skillet in the oven and roast until it reaches an internal temperature of 165°F, about 1 hour and 15 minutes. Transfer the chicken to a cutting board and let it rest for 10 minutes.

Cut the chickens and serve atop the roasted vegetables. Spoon the remaining pan gravy on top of the chicken.

CHICKEN GIZZARD GRILLADES WITH STONE-GROUND GRITS SERVES 6

2 pounds chicken gizzards

2 tablespoons Creole seasoning, plus more as needed

2 cups buttermilk

¼ cup hot sauce

Blended oil or vegetable oil, for frying

Chicken Dredge (page 213)

4 tablespoons unsalted butter

1 cup julienned onion

2 tablespoons all-purpose flour

½ cup Chicken Stock (page 209)

Kosher salt

Black pepper

Stone-Ground Grits (page 178), for serving

Preheat the oven to 375°F.

Place the gizzards in a large cast-iron Dutch oven and cover with water seasoned with 2 tablespoons Creole seasoning. Cover the Dutch oven and bake for 2 hours. The gizzards should be tender but not falling apart. Strain the gizzards and discard the liquid.

Transfer the gizzards to a bowl and top with the buttermilk and the hot sauce. Cover the bowl and refrigerate for at least 4 hours.

Strain the gizzards and discard the liquid.

Heat the oven to the lowest possible temperature.

Add enough oil to come halfway up the sides of a deep fryer or a Dutch oven and heat to 350°F. Line a plate with paper towels.

Pour the dredge into a bowl. Add the gizzards and toss to coat the gizzards thoroughly. Shake off the excess dredge.

Working in batches, if necessary, fry the gizzards in the hot oil until golden and an internal temperature of 165°F, 3 to 5 minutes, depending on the size of the gizzard. Drain the gizzards on the paper towel–lined plate and transfer the plate to the oven to keep warm.

Melt the butter in a 12-inch cast-iron skillet set over medium heat. Add the onion and cook until caramelized, 8 to 10 minutes. Add the flour and stir with a wooden spoon until the onion is thoroughly coated. Slowly stir in the stock. Season with salt, pepper, and Creole seasoning. Reduce the heat to low and simmer until the sauce is thick enough to coat the back of a wooden spoon, about 10 minutes.

Add the fried gizzards to the skillet and stir to coat them with the sauce.

Serve the gizzard grillades over the Stone-Ground Grits.

CHICKEN CLEMENCEAU SERVES 6

This classic New Orleans dish was a staple of some of the grand Creole restaurants of New Orleans. Unique ingredients such as tasso add the perfect touch of spice and smokiness that elevate this dish to Creole royalty. Tasso ham is a smoked, spiced, and cured meat, and is a staple of Louisiana cuisine.

Cast-Iron Seared Chicken Thighs (page 153)

3 tablespoon blended oil or vegetable oil, divided

4 ounces tasso, diced (can use diced ham for a substitute)

1 pound white button mushrooms, quartered

2 large potatoes peeled and diced

1 cup diced onion

2 medium shallots, minced

2 garlic cloves, minced

2 cups Chicken Stock (page 209)

Kosher salt

Black pepper

Creole seasoning

8 ounces fresh or frozen peas

½ cup (1 stick) unsalted butter, cut into cubes

Juice of 1 lemon

Prepare the chicken thighs. While they are in the oven, make the rest of the dish.

Heat 1 tablespoon of the oil in a 12-inch cast-iron skillet set over medium-high heat. When the oil shimmers add the tasso and cook until the fat has rendered out, 5 to 7 minutes.

Add the mushrooms in one layer and cook without moving until they are browned on one side, 3 to 5 minutes. Stir, then cook until they are fully golden brown, 3 to 5 minutes more. Use a slotted spoon to transfer the tasso and mushrooms to a bowl. Set aside.

Add the potatoes, onion, and the remaining 2 tablespoons of oil to the drippings in the pan and stir to coat thoroughly. Spread the potatoes out along the bottom of the pan in a single layer. Cook until the potatoes are tender and golden, stirring every 2 minutes, for 10 to 15 minutes.

Add the shallots and garlic and cook, stirring occasionally, until the shallots are translucent, about 3 minutes. Return the tasso and mushrooms to the pan.

Add the stock, and season with salt, pepper, and Creole seasoning. Stir, reduce the heat to medium, and cook until reduced by half, about 15 minutes.

Add the peas, stir, and cook until heated through, about 5 minutes if fresh, 2 minutes if frozen. Remove the pan from the heat.

Stir in the butter, 1 cube at a time. Do not add more butter until the piece before it has been incorporated. The sauce will thicken. Add the lemon juice and stir.

Arrange the vegetables and sauce on a large serving platter. Top with the chicken thighs and any juices and serve.

STEWED CHICKEN THIGHS SERVES 4

4 chicken thighs (about 1½ pounds), bone-in or boneless, with skin, trimmed of any excess skin or fat

2 tablespoons blended oil or vegetable oil, divided

1 tablespoon Creole seasoning

1 cup all-purpose flour

1 cup diced onion

2 garlic cloves, minced

2 tablespoons unsalted butter

2 cups Chicken Stock (page 209)

Kosher salt

Black pepper

Season the chicken with 1 tablespoon of oil and the Creole seasoning.

Pour the flour into a shallow bowl.

Heat the remaining 1 tablespoon of oil in a 10-inch cast-iron skillet set over medium heat. When the oil shimmers, dredge the skin side of the chicken through the flour, shake off the excess, and place the chicken, skin-side down, into the skillet. When the skin has turned golden brown, 6 to 8 minutes, turn the chicken and cook for another 4 minutes. Transfer the chicken to a plate.

To the same pan, still over medium-high heat, add the onion and stir with a wooden spoon, taking care to scrape the browned bits from the bottom of the pan. Add the garlic, stir, and cook until fragrant, about 1 minute. Add the butter and stir to combine. Add the stock and bring to a simmer.

Reduce the heat to medium-low and add the chicken and any juices that have accumulated back to the pan. Cook until the gravy is thick enough to coat the back of a wooden spoon and the chicken is cooked through to an internal temperature of 165°F, 25 to 30 minutes. Season with salt and pepper to taste.

CAST-IRON SEARED CHICKEN THIGHS SERVES 4 TO 6

6 chicken thighs, skin-on and bone-in

Creole seasoning

1 tablespoon blended oil or vegetable oil

Preheat the oven to 350°F.

Season the chicken with Creole seasoning.

Heat the oil in a 12-inch cast-iron skillet over medium-high heat until the oil shimmers. Add the chicken pieces to the skillet, skin-side down, and cook for 2 minutes. Reduce the heat to medium-low and continue cooking, skin-side down, occasionally rearranging the chicken thighs and rotating the pan to evenly distribute the heat, until the fat renders out and the skin is golden brown, about 12 minutes.

Transfer the skillet to the oven and cook for 13 minutes more. Flip the chicken pieces so they are skin-side up and continue cooking until the skin crisps and the meat is cooked through to an internal temperature of 165°F, about 5 minutes longer. Transfer to a plate and let rest for 5 minutes before serving.

SMOTHERED TURKEY NECKS SERVES 6

One of my favorite things about cooking is the simple joy of the aromas that can perfume the kitchen, and the entire house for that matter. When it's time to roast the holiday turkey, one of the most important steps is the making of that glorious gravy. Turkey necks provide the base for the gravy, and the process can be quite rewarding. It may not be something you have eaten before, but if the smell of the gravy that this recipe creates can't entice you, then you are truly missing out on one of deepest poultry flavors that you can experience.

2 pounds turkey necks

Kosher salt

Black pepper

2 tablespoons unsalted butter

2 cups thinly sliced onions

1 cup chopped celery

1 cup peeled and chopped carrots

2 tablespoons tomato paste

3 quarts Chicken Stock (page 209)

Deviled Egg Potato Salad (page 164), for serving

Preheat the oven to 400°F.

Season the turkey necks with salt and lots of black pepper.

Arrange the necks in a roasting pan large enough to hold them in a single layer (or work in batches) and roast for 25 minutes.

Transfer the necks to a plate.

Melt the butter in the roasting pan over medium heat. Add the onions, celery, carrots, and tomato paste, stir, and cook the vegetables until they are very soft and caramelized, about 10 minutes.

Add the stock and deglaze the pan using a wooden spoon to scrape the browned bits from the bottom. Cover and cook for 20 minutes. Remove the pan from the heat.

Add the turkey necks to the braising liquid. Cover the pan tightly with aluminum foil and bake for 1 hour and 15 minutes. The necks should be pull-apart tender.

Serve with the Deviled Egg Potato Salad.

VEGETABLES AND SIDES

In many New Orleans restaurants, some of our freshly prepared vegetables and sides have an almost cult-like following. They include fresh grilled corn with browned butter and Creole spices, Southern greens with bacon and sugarcane, and baked macaroni and red gravy, which should really be in its own food group. These side items can change a dinner from memorable to monumental all by themselves. Rest assured, there will be no calls to "eat your veggies" at the table.

BUTTERMILK BISCUITS MAKES 4 LARGE OR 8 TO 10 COCKTAIL-SIZE BISCUITS

Biscuits are thought of as a breakfast accompaniment with sweet jams or butter to start your day, but when you use them in a savory application, you can really take them to another level. Rich gravies or spicy fried chicken and sugarcane syrup can change the way you think about biscuits for dinner. Use this recipe to explore all the ways you have been missing out on these great Southern delights.

2 cups all-purpose flour

1½ tablespoons baking powder

1 teaspoon kosher salt

2 tablespoons sugar, plus more for sprinkling (omit for savory biscuits)

¼ cup heavy cream

1 cup buttermilk

Preheat the oven to 350°F. Line a baking sheet with parchment paper.

Combine the flour, baking powder, salt, 2 tablespoons of sugar, cream, and buttermilk in the bowl of a stand mixer fitted with a dough hook. Combine the dough at low speed until it pulls away from the bowl, scraping down the sides of the bowl with a spatula, as necessary. The dough should be stiff, yet tacky to the touch.

Scrape the dough onto a floured surface, knead it into a smooth ball, then roll it out into a 1-inch-thick mass. Use a 2-inch biscuit cutter to cut out large biscuits. For cocktail biscuits, use a 1-inch biscuit cutter.

Place the biscuits 2 inches apart on the prepared baking sheet. Sprinkle the tops lightly with sugar.

For large biscuits, bake for 7 minutes, rotate the baking sheet, and bake for 7 more minutes, or until just turning golden brown. For cocktail-size biscuits, check for doneness at 4 minutes.

SOUTHERN SPOON BREAD SERVES 12

With roots in Mesoamerican, Native American, and African cultures, spoon bread has evolved throughout history and has been linked to French influence as early as the 1700s when enslaved cooks were taught French recipes and techniques. With its golden color, it is said to bring good fortune and wealth to those who eat it and share it with friends. It's a Southern staple at the dinner table, and a must add to your family meals.

1⅓ cups all-purpose flour

1 cup cornmeal

¾ cup sugar

2 tablespoons baking powder

1 teaspoon kosher salt

¼ cup vegetable oil

2 whole eggs

¾ cup, plus 2 tablespoons whole milk

3 egg whites

Kernels from 2 ears corn (about 1 ½ cups)

Preheat the oven to 350° F. Butter a 9 x 13-inch glass baking dish.

Combine the flour, cornmeal, sugar, baking powder, and salt in a medium bowl and whisk to combine. Set aside.

In a separate bowl, combine the olive oil, eggs, and milk and whisk to combine. Then whisk the liquid mixture into the dry mixture, taking care to ensure the ingredients are thoroughly blended. Set aside.

In another bowl beat the egg whites with an electric mixer until stiff peaks form.

Use a spatula to gently fold the cornmeal mixture into the beaten egg whites. It is okay if a few white streaks remain. Gently fold in the corn. Transfer the mixture to the prepared baking dish.

Bake the spoon bread for 10 minutes. Rotate the dish and cook until the top puffs and turns light golden brown, about 10 minutes more. Let cool for 5 minutes to set up before serving it with a big spoon.

SOUTHERN-STYLE CORNBREAD SERVES 12

My mother used to bake our cornbread in a cast-iron skillet. If you choose to bake it that way, put the skillet in the oven while it preheats, and then melt a couple of tablespoons of butter in the hot skillet before adding the batter.

1⅓ cups all-purpose flour

1 cup cornmeal

¾ cup sugar

2 tablespoons baking powder

1¼ teaspoons kosher salt

¼ cup vegetable oil

2 large eggs

¾ cup, plus 2 tablespoons whole milk

Preheat the oven to 350° F. Butter a 9 x 13-inch glass baking dish.

Combine the flour, cornmeal, sugar, baking powder, and salt in a medium bowl and whisk to combine. Set aside.

In a separate bowl, combine the olive oil, eggs, and milk and whisk to combine. Then whisk the liquid mixture into the dry mixture, taking care to ensure the ingredients are thoroughly blended. Transfer the mixture into the prepared baking dish.

Bake for 10 minutes. Rotate the dish and continue to bake until the top puffs and turns light golden brown, about 10 minutes more. Let cool for 5 minutes before serving.

SMOTHERED POTATOES SERVES 6

2 pounds small Red Bliss potatoes, cut in half

Kosher salt

4 tablespoons unsalted butter, divided

1 large onion, cut in half and thinly sliced

¼ cup chopped Italian flat-leaf parsley

½ teaspoon Creole seasoning, plus more as needed

Black pepper

Combine the potatoes and enough salted water to cover in a large pot over medium-high heat and bring to a boil. Cook until the potatoes are fork tender, about 15 minutes. Drain and set the potatoes aside.

Melt 2 tablespoons of butter in a 10-inch cast-iron skillet over low heat. Add the onion and cook, stirring frequently, until caramelized, about 15 minutes.

Add the reserved potatoes and the remaining 2 tablespoons of butter and mix. Add the parsley and the Creole seasoning. Taste and season with salt, pepper, and more Creole seasoning if desired.

HOME-STYLE MASHED POTATOES SERVES 6

8 large Yukon Gold potatoes, peeled and cut into large dice

Kosher salt

1½ cups (3 sticks) cold unsalted butter, cut into cubes

½ to ¾ cup hot whole milk

White pepper

Combine the potatoes with enough salted water to cover in a large saucepan over medium-high heat. Cook the potatoes until fork tender, 25 to 30 minutes. Drain.

Ideally, pass the potatoes through a ricer or food mill. If unavailable, return the potatoes to the pot and mash them with a handheld masher as desired.

Add the butter, a few cubes at a time, and mix well. Add the milk in small quantities until it reaches the desired consistency.

Season with salt and pepper as desired, and serve while hot.

<< Smothered Potatoes

DEVILED EGG POTATO SALAD SERVES 8

Kosher salt

3 pounds russet potatoes, peeled and diced into 1-inch pieces

2 cups mayonnaise

½ cup Creole mustard

¼ cup Dijon mustard

¼ cup yellow mustard

1 cup diced white onion

1 cup finely diced celery

¼ cup sliced green onions

12 hard-boiled eggs, peeled

Boil the potatoes in a pot of salted water over medium-high heat until they are soft but not mushy, about 10 minutes. Drain and set aside.

In a large bowl, combine the mayonnaise and mustards and mix thoroughly with a rubber spatula.

Add the potatoes, onion, celery, green onion, and the eggs to the bowl.

Use the spatula to break up the eggs into irregular-size pieces then gently fold everything together.

Serve warm or cold.

HOLIDAY SWEET POTATOES WITH CANDIED PECANS SERVES 6

5 large sweet potatoes

5 tablespoons unsalted butter, softened

2½ tablespoons light brown sugar

¾ teaspoon vanilla extract

Pinch nutmeg

Kosher salt

Candied Pecans (recipe follows)

Preheat the oven to 350°F.

Bake the sweet potatoes until they are soft, 1 to 1½ hours. Cool thoroughly. Scoop out the potato flesh into a large bowl and discard the skins.

Add the butter, brown sugar, vanilla, and nutmeg and stir and mash the mixture. Transfer the mixture to an 8 x 8-inch baking dish. Top with the Candied Pecans. Cover with aluminum foil and bake for 20 minutes. Remove from the oven and peel back the foil being careful of the steam. Serve hot.

CANDIED PECANS MAKES 1 POUND

Pecan trees are native to the southern United States and Northern Mexico and thrive in temperate climates. Besides the standard application in pies and desserts, pecans can be a delicious addition to seasonal salads. Try this recipe out and discover new ways to enjoy this delicious treat.

1⅔ cups light Karo corn syrup

½ cup sugar

1 pound Louisiana pecan halves

Blended oil or vegetable oil, for frying

In a large, deep saucepan over medium-high heat, combine the corn syrup, sugar, and 1⅔ cups water and stir well. Cook, stirring often, until the sugar has dissolved.

Bring the mixture to a boil, add the pecans, and boil, stirring constantly to keep the pecans from floating to the top, for 10 minutes.

Strain the pecans over a bowl. Set the pecans aside. After cooling, the leftover syrup can be retained in an airtight container for up to 7 days. You can use it to make another batch of candied pecans, or as a biscuit topper for breakfast treats.

Prepare a deep fryer with oil coming halfway up the sides and heat the oil to 350°F. Line a baking sheet with paper towels.

Fry the pecans in the hot oil until they are brick red, about 30 seconds. Use a strainer or slotted spoon to remove the pecans and drain on the paper towel–lined baking sheet. The pecans will continue to darken by two shades. Cool to room temperature. Store in an airtight container in the refrigerator for up to 7 days.

SMOTHERED GREEN BEANS SERVES 6

2 tablespoons unsalted butter

6 thick slices bacon, diced

1 small onion, thinly sliced

1½ pounds fresh green beans, trimmed

½ cup Chicken Stock (page 209)

Kosher salt

Black pepper

Melt the butter in a 12-inch cast-iron pan over medium heat. Add the bacon and cook until the fat has rendered, 4 to 5 minutes. Add the onion and cook until it is a caramel color, about 6 minutes.

Add the green beans and stock, reduce the heat to low, and cook until the green beans are crisp-tender, 3 to 5 minutes. Season with salt and pepper and serve while hot.

GERMAN RED CABBAGE MAKES ABOUT 3 CUPS

2 tablespoons blended oil or vegetable oil

1 medium red onion, thinly sliced

1 small head red cabbage, shredded (6 to 8 cups)

½ cup sugar

1 cup apple cider vinegar

1 teaspoon kosher salt

¼ teaspoon black pepper

2 tablespoons balsamic vinegar

⅛ teaspoon ground cinnamon

⅛ teaspoon ground cloves

Heat the oil in a small cast-iron Dutch oven set over medium heat. Add the onion, stir, and cook until soft, about 5 minutes. Add the cabbage, sugar, cider vinegar, salt, pepper, balsamic vinegar, cinnamon, and cloves. Stir, cover, reduce the heat to low, and cook until the cabbage is soft, about 45 minutes. Serve hot as a side dish.

Smothered Green Beans >>

SUMMER CORN MAQUE CHOUX SERVES 6

2 tablespoons blended oil or vegetable oil

2 cups diced onions

1 cup diced celery

1 cup diced green bell pepper

1 (28-ounce) can crushed tomatoes, with their juice

Kernels from 6 large ears corn

2 cups sliced okra, optional

½ cup (1 stick) unsalted butter, cut into cubes

1 tablespoon Creole seasoning, plus more as needed

Heat the oil in a large cast-iron Dutch oven set over medium heat. When the oil shimmers, add the onions, celery, and bell pepper and cook the vegetables until they have softened, about 10 minutes.

Add the tomatoes and cook, stirring often, for 15 minutes.

Add the corn and okra, if using, and cook until the liquid has reduced by one third, 10 to 12 minutes.

Reduce the heat to low and add the butter, stirring constantly until melted. Add the Creole seasoning, taste, and add more as desired. Serve hot as a side dish.

<< Served with Cast-Iron Seared Chicken Thighs (page 153)

SOUTHERN BRAISED GREENS SERVES 6

1 cup chopped bacon

1 large onion, diced

3 bunches fresh greens, collard, mustard, or a mixture, thoroughly washed, stemmed, torn or shredded

1½ tablespoons Steen's cane syrup

3 tablespoons Steen's cane vinegar

Kosher salt

Black pepper

Cook the bacon in a 12-inch cast-iron skillet set over medium-high heat. When the fat has rendered from the bacon, add the onion and cook until translucent, 5 to 7 minutes.

Add 1 cup of water. Begin adding the greens in batches, stirring until all greens have been added. Cover the skillet with a tight-fitting lid and cook, stirring occasionally, until the greens are fully wilted and tender, 35 to 40 minutes.

Remove the skillet from the heat. Stir in the syrup, vinegar, salt, and pepper and serve.

SMOTHERED OKRA AND TOMATOES SERVES 6

4 tablespoons unsalted butter, divided

½ cup chopped onion

¼ cup chopped green bell pepper

¼ cup chopped celery

2 tablespoons minced garlic

4 cups sliced okra

6 ripe tomatoes, diced, with their juice

Kosher salt

Black pepper

Creole seasoning

Melt 2 tablespoons of butter in a 12-inch cast-iron skillet over medium heat. Add the onion, bell pepper, and celery and cook the vegetables until they are soft, 5 to 7 minutes.

Add the garlic, stir, and cook until fragrant, about 1 minute. Add the okra and tomatoes, stir, and cook until the mixture has thickened slightly, 20 to 25 minutes.

Remove the skillet from the heat. Add the remaining 2 tablespoons butter and stir until the butter has melted. Season with salt, pepper, and Creole seasoning.

MACARONI PIE WITH CREOLE RED GRAVY SERVES 8

1 tablespoon kosher salt

2 (12-ounce) boxes dried bucatini pasta

Unsalted butter, for greasing the baking dish

10 cups (2½ quarts) heavy cream

4 large eggs

5 cups shredded cheddar cheese, divided

½ teaspoon ground white pepper

Creole Red Gravy (recipe follows)

Bring a large pot of water seasoned with the salt to a boil over medium-high heat. Add the dry bucatini and cook until al dente, about 7 minutes. Drain but do not rinse.

Preheat the oven to 375°F. Butter a large casserole dish.

Transfer the cooked bucatini to the baking dish.

Heat the cream in a large cast-iron Dutch oven set over medium-low heat. While the cream is heating, whisk the eggs in a medium bowl.

When the cream is just warm to the touch, temper the eggs by adding a large ladle of warm cream to the eggs while whisking constantly. Add the tempered eggs to the cream in the pot and whisk to combine. Add 4 cups of the cheese and the white pepper to the custard, increase the heat to medium, and whisk until the cheese has melted.

Ladle the cheese custard over the cooked bucatini. Use a spatula to ensure the custard is thoroughly coating the noodles and to force the coated pasta into the corners of the baking dish. Smooth out the top. Cover the casserole with the remaining cheese.

Bake for about 30 minutes, or until golden, bubbly, and thick.

Allow the casserole to cool and set up, 15 to 20 minutes. Cut the casserole into 8 squares and serve.

continued >>

CREOLE RED GRAVY MAKES 2½ QUARTS

2 tablespoons blended oil or vegetable oil

2 teaspoons red pepper flakes

1 cup finely diced onion

½ cup finely diced celery

½ cup finely diced green bell pepper

3 tablespoons tomato paste

1 tablespoon chopped garlic

1 (36-ounce) can diced tomatoes, with juices

½ cup Beef Stock (page 211) or Chicken Stock (page 209)

1 bay leaf

Kosher salt

Heat the oil in a large cast-iron Dutch oven set over medium heat. Add the pepper flakes and cook, stirring constantly, until the oil is the color of saffron.

Add the onion, celery, and bell pepper and cook, stirring often, until the vegetables have softened, 5 to 7 minutes.

Add the tomato paste and stir to coat the vegetables. Continue cooking until deeply caramelized, about 8 minutes. Add the garlic, stir to combine, and cook until fragrant, about 1 minute.

Add the tomatoes, 1 cup water, stock, and bay leaf, bring the sauce to a simmer, and cook, stirring occasionally, until the sauce has thickened and the vegetables have broken down, about 30 minutes. Remove the bay leaf before serving. Spoon the gravy on top or place on the side of the baked macaroni to serve. Leftover gravy can be cooled and stored in an airtight container in the refrigerator for up to 5 days.

MASCARPONE POLENTA SERVES 6

1 tablespoon kosher salt, plus more as needed

1 cup yellow Italian polenta (may substitute stone-ground grits)

8 ounces mascarpone cheese (may substitute cream cheese)

Combine 4 cups of water and the salt and bring to a boil in a medium saucepan over medium-high heat.

Add the polenta, stir, and reduce the heat to the lowest possible setting. Cook, stirring often, for 20 minutes. If the polenta is too tight, rather than creamy, add more water, 1 tablespoon at a time.

Whisk in the mascarpone. Season with salt.

STONE-GROUND GRITS SERVES 6

3 cups whole milk

Kosher salt

Black pepper

8 tablespoons (1 stick) unsalted butter, divided

2 cups white or yellow stone-ground grits

Combine 3 cups of water with the milk, salt, pepper, and 4 table-spoons of butter in a medium saucepan or Dutch oven over medium-high heat and bring to a low boil.

Reduce the heat to low, slowly add the grits, stirring constantly, and cook until the liquid is absorbed, about 30 minutes.

Stir in the remaining 4 tablespoons butter. Remove from the heat when grits are fully cooked and creamy without a crunch.

Mascarpone Polenta >>

DIRTY RICE SERVES 6

2 tablespoons unsalted butter

⅔ cup minced onion

⅓ cup minced celery

½ cup minced green bell pepper

2 tablespoons minced garlic

½ teaspoon dried thyme

1¼ teaspoons ground cumin

8 ounces puréed chicken livers

1½ pounds ground pork

1½ cups parboiled (converted) rice

1 (12-ounce) bottle lager beer

2½ cups Chicken Stock (page 209)

2 bay leaves

Kosher salt

Black pepper

Sliced green onions, for garnish

Melt the butter in a 12-inch cast-iron skillet over medium heat. Add the onion, celery, and bell pepper and cook the vegetables until they are fully softened but not caramelized, 10 to 15 minutes.

Add the garlic, thyme, and cumin, stir, and cook until fragrant, about 1 minute. Add the ground pork and the livers and cook, stirring frequently, for about 10 minutes.

Add the rice and stir well. Add the beer, stock, and bay leaves, cover the pot with a tight-fitting lid, and reduce the heat to the lowest setting. Cook for 20 minutes. Remove from the heat and fluff with a fork. Remove the bay leaves, and season with salt and pepper. Serve, garnished with green onions.

SHRIMP AND MIRLITON DRESSING SERVES 6

6 tablespoons unsalted butter

4 medium mirlitons, peeled, seeds discarded and cut into medium dice

1 cup diced onion

⅔ cup diced celery

⅔ cup diced green bell pepper

2 bay leaves

1½ tablespoons minced garlic

½ cup Chicken Stock (page 209)

1½ pounds (21- to 25-count) shrimp, peeled, deveined, and cut in half

1 to 2 cups unseasoned breadcrumbs

½ cup grated Parmesan cheese

Kosher salt

Black pepper

Preheat the oven to 350°F. Grease an 8 x 8-inch baking dish.

Melt the butter in a 12-inch cast-iron skillet over medium heat. Add the mirlitons, onion, celery, bell pepper, and bay leaves and cook the vegetables until they are fully softened but not caramelized, about 10 minutes.

Reduce the heat to medium-low, add the garlic, and cook until aromatic, about 1 minute. Add the stock and shrimp and cook until the shrimp are just pink, about 4 minutes.

Add 1 cup of breadcrumbs and stir to combine. Add additional breadcrumbs if necessary to achieve the desired consistency.

Stir in the Parmesan cheese, and season with salt and pepper. Remove the bay leaves.

Transfer the dressing to the prepared baking dish and bake until golden and bubbly, 25 to 30 minutes, or if you prefer, you can just bake the dressing in the cast-iron skillet. Serve while hot as a side dish.

MÉMÈRE'S HOLIDAY OYSTER DRESSING SERVES 6

Many of these recipes come straight from my family, and this one in particular is what I love most from my grandmother. Our French roots in Louisiana have many of us still calling our grandparents mémère and pépère and many of us call our godparents nanny and paran. Almost anyone who is a close friend of your parents is an aunt or uncle, and kids you grew up close to are all cousins. That says a lot about how important family is in our community. It's not just blood.

1 quart oysters, with their liquid

½ cup (1 stick) unsalted butter

½ cup chopped bacon

1 cup chopped onion

½ cup chopped green bell pepper

½ cup chopped celery

1 tablespoon chopped garlic

¼ cup chopped Italian flat-leaf parsley

Creole seasoning

2 cups breadcrumbs

Preheat the oven to 350°F. Grease an 8 x 8-inch baking dish.

Pour the oysters and their liquid into a food processor and pulse 4 or 5 times to break the oysters up a bit but not to liquefy. Set aside.

Melt the butter in a medium cast-iron Dutch oven over medium heat. Add the bacon and cook until the fat is rendered, 8 to 10 minutes. Add the onion, bell pepper, and celery and cook until the onion is translucent, about 10 minutes. Add the garlic and cook until fragrant, about 1 minute.

Add the reserved oysters and the parsley and stir to combine. Reduce the heat to low and season with Creole seasoning. Simmer the oyster mixture for 10 minutes.

Starting with ¼ cup, add enough breadcrumbs to achieve a thick consistency.

Transfer the mixture to the prepared baking dish and bake until golden and bubbly, about 30 minutes. Serve while hot as a side dish.

ANDOUILLE AND CORNBREAD DRESSING SERVES 6

1 cup small-diced andouille sausage

2 tablespoons unsalted butter

½ cup diced onion

¼ cup diced green bell pepper

¼ cup diced celery

1 tablespoon minced garlic

½ teaspoon Creole seasoning

½ teaspoon kosher salt

Pinch black pepper

2 cups Chicken Stock (page 209), plus more as needed

4 cups crumbled Southern-Style Cornbread (page 160)

Preheat the oven to 350°F. Grease an 8 x 8-inch baking dish.

Combine the andouille and butter in a 12-inch cast-iron skillet set over medium heat. When the fat has rendered out of the sausage, add the onion, bell pepper, and celery and cook, stirring frequently, until the vegetables have softened and begun to caramelize, about 8 minutes.

Add the garlic and cook until fragrant, about 1 minute. Add the Creole seasoning and salt and stir.

Add 2 cups of stock and deglaze the pan, using a flat-edged wooden spoon to scrape the brown bits from the bottom.

Add the crumbled cornbread and stir to blend thoroughly. Add additional stock as necessary to create a thick consistency.

Transfer the mixture to the prepared baking dish and bake until golden and bubbling, about 30 minutes. Serve while hot as a side dish

DESSERTS AND
SWEET TREATS

The end of the meal is by no means any less important than the beginning, especially in the South. The key is to keep it simple and let the ingredients speak for themselves. Maybe add a little shot of your favorite liquor or Champagne if that's your thing. We tend to add liquor to everything down South, so a little shot in your dessert is pretty common. Dessert in New Orleans is often accompanied by a delicious cordial or a robust cup of coffee—both serve the purpose of continuing the conversation and enjoying the company around the table. So, use these recipes to enjoy whatever fruit or locally grown yummies that are available to you, and keep the conversation going.

BROWN BUTTER, SEA SALT, AND CHOCOLATE CHUNK COOKIES MAKES 12 TO 15 COOKIES

1 cup (2 sticks) unsalted butter

¾ cup sugar

2 eggs

1 teaspoon vanilla extract

½ cup plus 2 tablespoons dark brown sugar

2 cups all-purpose flour

1½ teaspoons baking soda

1 teaspoon kosher salt

2 cups semisweet chocolate chunks

Sea salt flakes

Melt the butter in a small saucepan over medium-high heat, stirring constantly, until the butter starts to foam up. It will sizzle and smell nutty in about 4 minutes. Once the butter looks foamy and it stops sizzling, about 2 minutes more, remove it from the heat. It will be golden brown. Pour it into a bowl and refrigerate until soft but not solid, 30 to 40 minutes.

Preheat the oven to 350°F. Line two baking sheets with parchment paper or liberally spray with nonstick cooking spray.

In a large bowl, whisk together the sugar, eggs, and vanilla until the mixture is white and creamy. Add the brown sugar and mix thoroughly.

In a separate bowl, combine the flour, baking soda, and salt. Add the flour mixture to the sugar mixture and mix well. Fold in the chocolate chunks.

Use a cookie scoop or tablespoon to scoop the cookie dough onto the prepared baking sheets. Sprinkle generously with sea salt.

Bake for 5½ minutes, rotate the pans, then bake for 5½ minutes more, or until the cookies are lightly golden, soft in the center, and crisp on the edges.

Transfer the cookies to a wire rack with a metal spatula to cool.

SPICED WHISKEY AND APPLE COBBLER
WITH SNICKERDOODLE COOKIE CRUMBLE SERVES 6

FOR THE COBBLER

½ teaspoon ground cloves

1 teaspoon ground cinnamon

1 teaspoon ground nutmeg

½ teaspoon ground star anise

3 tablespoons unsalted butter

4 Granny Smith apples,
  peeled, cored, and sliced
  ¼ inch thick

⅓ cup whiskey

½ teaspoon kosher salt

½ cup dark brown sugar

¼ cup sugar

2 tablespoons cornstarch

2 teaspoons vanilla extract

Juice of 1 lemon

FOR THE SNICKERDOODLE COOKIE CRUMBLE

½ cup (1 stick) unsalted
  butter, softened

¾ cup plus 2 tablespoons
  sugar, divided

1 egg

1 teaspoon baking powder

¼ teaspoon kosher salt

1⅔ cups all-purpose flour

1½ teaspoons ground
  cinnamon

COBBLER

Combine the cloves, cinnamon, nutmeg, and star anise in a small bowl. Set aside.

Melt the butter in a medium saucepan over medium-low heat. Add the apples, whiskey, salt, sugars, cornstarch, and reserved spice blend and mix well.

Add the vanilla and lemon juice and cook, stirring often, until the apples have softened slightly, about 5 minutes.

Transfer the apple mixture to an 8 x 8-inch baking pan. Set aside.

Preheat the oven to 350°F.

COOKIE CRUMBLE

In a large bowl, mash together the butter and ¾ cup of sugar. Add the egg and beat until creamy. Add the baking powder, salt, and flour and stir to make a stiff dough.

In a small bowl, combine the cinnamon and the remaining 2 tablespoons sugar. Shape the dough into balls the size of a walnut. Roll them in the cinnamon-sugar mixture.

TO ASSEMBLE

Break the cookie dough balls into small pieces over the apple filling. Bake the cobbler until the top is golden, about 13 minutes. Serve warm.

VANILLA MAGIC CAKE WITH MACERATED STRAWBERRIES SERVES 6

The magic cake is a French dessert known as gâteau magique. With a low baking temperature, it magically forms three distinct and texturally different layers. Sponge cake on top, a cream layer in the middle, and a custard/flan layer on the bottom. This is a simple cake, yet fun and unique.

4 large eggs, separated

1¼ cups powdered sugar, plus more for dusting

½ cup (1 stick) unsalted butter, melted and slightly cooled

1 cup all-purpose flour

2 cups lukewarm whole milk

2 teaspoons vanilla extract

1 pint strawberries, washed, hulled, and sliced

3 tablespoons sugar

Whipped cream, optional, for serving

Preheat the oven to 325°F. Lightly grease an 8 x 8-inch baking dish.

In a large bowl, whip the egg whites with an electric mixer until stiff peaks form. Set aside.

In another bowl, beat the egg yolks and the powdered sugar until pale yellow.

Temper the egg yolk mixture by rapidly whisking in 1 tablespoon of the melted butter. Drizzle in the rest of the butter while whisking constantly. Whisk in 1 tablespoon water and whip until evenly combined.

Add the flour and mix. Slowly beat in the milk and vanilla until well combined. Fold in the egg whites, about one third at a time.

Pour the batter into the prepared baking dish and bake until the cake is light golden but still slightly soft at the center, 40 to 60 minutes. Times will vary based on your oven, so start checking after 30 minutes. If the top browns too quickly and the center is still wet, cover the cake with aluminum foil and return it to the oven.

Cool the cake completely then dust with powdered sugar. The cake will remain soft due to the custard layer in the center.

In a small bowl, combine the strawberries and the sugar. Set aside to macerate for at least 10 minutes.

Serve the cake with the strawberries and whipped cream, if desired.

STICKY BUN BREAD PUDDING SERVES 12

Bread pudding is one of the more popular desserts in New Orleans, and you will find it on almost every menu in the city. Soaking the bread overnight is highly recommended and allows for the mixture to really come together before baking. There are many varieties served in Southern homes and restaurants that include additions like raisins or fresh seasonal berries. My mom still gives me grief about leaving out the raisins in my version, but I personally hate them and so do my sisters. Find your favorite combination and make it a special treat for your family and friends.

FOR THE BREAD PUDDING

7 (8-inch) loaves French bread, cubed

4 eggs

½ cup sugar

1 cup light brown sugar

3 tablespoons ground cinnamon

½ teaspoon kosher salt

1 quart whole milk

½ cup (1 stick) unsalted butter, melted

FOR THE TOPPING

½ cup (1 stick) unsalted butter

1 cup packed light brown sugar

2 tablespoons ground cinnamon

BREAD PUDDING

Place the bread cubes in a large bowl. Set aside. In a separate bowl, combine the eggs, sugars, cinnamon, and salt and whisk until well combined.

Slowly add the milk, whisking constantly, until fully incorporated to make a custard. Pour the custard over the bread cubes and use a rubber spatula to press the bread into the custard until it is saturated. Add the butter and mix again until the butter is evenly distributed. Let the bread soak for a minimum of 12 to 24 hours, covered and refrigerated.

Preheat the oven to 350°F. Grease a 9 x 13-inch baking dish, and place the bread pudding mixture into the dish.

TOPPING

Melt the butter in a small saucepan over medium-high heat. Add the brown sugar and cinnamon and whisk constantly until the mixture starts to bubble. Continue whisking for 2 minutes.

ASSEMBLY

While the butter mixture is hot, pour it over the bread pudding and spread it evenly. Cover the dish with aluminum foil and bake for 35 minutes.

Remove the foil and continue baking until the custard is set and the topping is browned, bubbling, and sticky, about 25 minutes.

Allow the bread pudding to set up and cool for at least 30 minutes before serving warm.

Note: I frequently make a second batch of the topping to spoon over the warm bread pudding served with vanilla ice cream.

SPICED SWEET POTATO BEIGNETS SERVES 6

Beignets date back to the seventeenth century, and the consumption of fried dough goes back for centuries. The beignet was brought to America by French settlers and by the Acadians. Famous spots like Café Du Monde in New Orleans offer the traditional fried pastry with powdered sugar and a hot café au lait on the side. The use of sweet potato in this recipe is a fun way to add some sweetness to the menu around the holidays. I like to add sugarcane syrup to mine for some added flavor.

3 cups all-purpose flour

1 cup buttermilk

1 cup whole milk

1 large egg

2 tablespoons baking powder

½ teaspoon ground cinnamon

2 teaspoons sugar

1 teaspoon kosher salt

1 medium sweet potato, peeled and finely grated

3 cups vegetable oil, for frying

Powdered sugar, for dusting

Combine the flour, buttermilk, milk, egg, baking powder, cinnamon, sugar, and salt in a large bowl and mix until smooth. Fold in the grated sweet potato.

Pour the oil into a deep fryer, deep skillet, or Dutch oven and heat over medium-high heat to 360°F. Line a baking sheet with paper towels.

Drop tablespoons of the batter into the hot oil and fry, turning once. The beignets are ready when they rise to the surface and turn golden brown and puffy, 3 to 5 minutes per batch. Drain on the paper towel–lined baking sheet.

Dust lightly with the powdered sugar and serve.

CRÊPES SUZETTE SERVES 6

3 eggs

1½ cups (3 sticks) unsalted butter, half melted and half softened

1½ cups whole milk

1½ teaspoons vanilla extract

¾ teaspoon kosher salt

1¾ cups all-purpose flour

Blended oil or vegetable oil, for greasing the skillet

¾ cup sugar

½ cup fresh orange juice

4 tablespoons brandy

Combine the eggs, the melted butter, milk, vanilla, ⅓ cup water, salt, and flour in a blender and blend until smooth. The batter should be thick enough to lightly coat a spoon. If it is too thick, add a little more water and blend again.

Lightly grease a small skillet with a paper towel dipped in the oil. Set the skillet over medium heat. When the oil shimmers, use a small ladle to add enough batter to thinly cover the bottom of the pan. When the edge of the crêpe turns brown and small holes appear, about 1 minute, turn the crêpe and cook for about 30 seconds longer.

Turn the crêpe out onto a paper towel and repeat the process until all the batter is used. Set 12 crêpes aside. The remainder can be frozen between sheets of wax paper to use later.

Combine the remaining softened butter and the sugar in a large nonstick skillet over medium heat. Cook, stirring, until the sugar is caramelized and the color of amber, about 4 minutes. Add the orange juice, a little at a time, and continue stirring until all the juice has been added and the mixture is smooth. Reduce the heat to a simmer.

Fold each crêpe in half and then in half again to form triangles. Add the folded crêpes to the sauce in the skillet and spoon the sauce over each crêpe. Add the brandy and ignite it carefully with a long match. Spoon the flaming sauce over the folded crêpes until the flames burn out.

Serve 2 crêpes per person with some of the sauce.

PONCHATOULA STRAWBERRY SHORTCAKE AND CHANTILLY CRÈME SERVES 4

Strawberries from Ponchatoula, about an hour's drive northwest of New Orleans, are large and ruby-colored. When you can smell them as they ripen in the sun, you know spring is close. This is a dish my daughter fell in love with during my time at Commander's Palace, and she would always ask for it at home. To this day, it is always the most requested dessert at our house.

Buttermilk Biscuits (page 158)

1 pint fresh strawberries, hulled and quartered

⅓ cup sugar

1 tablespoon Malibu dark coconut rum

Chantilly Crème (recipe follows)

Make the biscuits and set them aside to cool.

Combine the strawberries, sugar, and rum in a small bowl. Set aside.

When the biscuits are cool enough to handle, split them in half. Spoon the strawberries with juice over the bottom halves of the biscuits. Top with Chantilly Crème, then the biscuit tops. Serve.

CHANTILLY CRÈME MAKES ABOUT 2 CUPS

1 cup heavy cream, chilled

1½ teaspoons vanilla extract

2½ tablespoons powdered sugar

In a medium bowl, beat the cream, vanilla, and powdered sugar together with an electric mixer on high speed until stiff peaks form.

CLASSIC LEMON ICEBOX PIE SERVES 6 TO 8

14 graham crackers, broken

¼ cup sugar

¼ teaspoon kosher salt

6 tablespoons unsalted butter, melted

2 (14-ounce) cans sweetened condensed milk

1 ¼ cups fresh lemon juice

2 tablespoons finely grated lemon zest

8 large egg yolks

Whipped cream, for serving

Preheat the oven to 325°F.

In a food processor, pulse the graham crackers with the sugar and salt until finely ground but not powdery. Add the butter and pulse until blended.

Transfer the mixture to a 9-inch springform pan and press the crumb mixture into the bottom and two-thirds up the sides of the pan. Use a small straight-side juice glass to help in pressing the crumbs evenly. Set the pan on a rimmed baking sheet.

In a medium bowl, whisk the condensed milk with the lemon juice. In another bowl use an electric hand mixer to beat the lemon zest with the egg yolks until pale. Pour this into the condensed milk mixture and beat until smooth. Pour the filling into the crust.

Bake the pie for 25 minutes, or until the center jiggles slightly and the edges are set. Transfer the springform pan to a wire rack and cool for 1 hour.

Loosely cover the pan with plastic wrap and freeze the pie for at least 6 hours.

To serve, wrap a warm, damp kitchen towel around the sides of the springform pan to release the pie, then remove the outer ring. Use a hot knife to cut the pie in slices. Serve with whipped cream.

CHERRIES JUBILEE SERVES 6

½ cup sugar

2 tablespoons cornstarch

¼ cup freshly squeezed orange juice

1 pound Bing or other dark, sweet cherries, rinsed and pitted

½ teaspoon finely grated orange zest

6 scoops vanilla ice cream

¼ teaspoon cherry extract

¼ cup brandy

Whisk the sugar and cornstarch together in a wide saucepan. Stir in ¼ cup cold water and the orange juice and bring to a boil over medium-high heat, whisking until thickened, about 4 minutes.

Stir in the cherries and the orange zest and return to a boil. Reduce the heat to medium-low and simmer for 10 minutes to allow the cherries to soften.

While the cherries are cooking, spoon the ice cream into serving bowls.

Remove the pan from the heat and stir in the cherry extract. Pour in the brandy and use a long lighter to light it. Shake the pan until the blue flame has extinguished. Spoon the cherries and sauce over the ice cream to serve.

BANANAS FOSTER SERVES 6

This storied dessert was created by Chef Paul Blangé at Brennan's Restaurant in 1951. The name comes from Richard Foster, a restaurateur and founder of Brennan's Restaurant in the French Quarter. Brennen's still serves this famous dessert, flambéed table-side.

6 tablespoons unsalted butter

1½ cups dark brown sugar

¾ teaspoon ground cinnamon

⅓ cup banana liqueur

6 ripe firm bananas, peeled, cut in half lengthwise, then halved crosswise

⅓ cup dark rum

6 scoops vanilla ice cream

Combine the butter, brown sugar, and cinnamon in a skillet over low heat and cook, stirring, until the sugar dissolves. Stir in the banana liqueur, place the bananas in the pan and cook until the banana sections soften and begin to brown, 3 to 5 minutes.

Carefully add the rum and continue to cook the sauce until the rum is hot. Tip the pan slightly and ignite the rum with a long match.

When the flames subside, lift the bananas out of the pan and place 4 pieces over each portion of ice cream. Spoon the sauce over the top of the ice cream and serve.

SALAD DRESSINGS, STOCKS, AND DREDGES

This chapter truly captures the essence and the simplicity of Creole cooking. The devil is in the details. It's the little things that make the big difference. These seemingly simple recipes are what drives the spirit of cooks for generations. Seasonal ingredients and local inspiration can create memorable dining experiences.

HOMEMADE RANCH MAKES ABOUT 5 CUPS

2 cups sour cream

1½ cups mayonnaise

3 teaspoons celery salt

2 tablespoons garlic powder

1½ cups buttermilk

In a large bowl, combine the sour cream, mayonnaise, celery salt, and garlic powder.

While whisking, slowly add the buttermilk until you have a thick but pourable dressing.

Store in the refrigerator for up to 7 days. With caviar added, it will hold for 2 days.

NOTE: To make Caviar Ranch Dressing, add 1 teaspoon Cajun Caviar for each cup of dressing

SUGARCANE VINAIGRETTE MAKES 3½ CUPS

Two of my favorite ingredients in the kitchen are, without a doubt, Steen's sugarcane syrup and Steen's sugarcane vinegar. You absolutely have to put these two items in your everyday pantry. Their story is one of overcoming adversity and pushing forward with what is given to you. From near devastation of the cane crop due to an early winter freeze in 1910, Charley Steen salvaged his frozen crop into a few barrels of syrup, and as they say, the rest is history. The Steen family is still producing cane syrup and other products that can be found online and in the greatest kitchens in the world.

¾ cup Steen's cane syrup

¾ cup Steen's cane vinegar

2 teaspoons Dijon mustard

2 teaspoons black pepper

2 cups vegetable oil

Kosher salt

Combine the cane syrup, vinegar, mustard, and black pepper in a food processor or blender and blend on high to combine. With the processor or blender running, stream in the oil through the feeding tube in the top until fully incorporated and the dressing has emulsified. Season with salt to taste. Store in the refrigerator for up to 7 days.

CREOLE MUSTARD VINAIGRETTE MAKES ABOUT 4½ CUPS

2 tablespoons minced onion

2 tablespoons minced green bell pepper

½ cup Steen's cane vinegar

1½ cups Creole mustard

¼ cup local honey

2 cups vegetable oil

Kosher salt

Black pepper

Combine the onion, bell pepper, and vinegar in a food processor or blender and process until smooth. Add the mustard and honey and process until blended.

With the processor or blender running, stream in the oil through the feeding tube in the top until the dressing has emulsified. Season with salt and pepper to taste. Store in the refrigerator for up to 7 days.

CITRUS VINAIGRETTE MAKES ABOUT 3 CUPS

Citrus trees thrive in Plaquemines Parish, which is just a ferry ride away from where I grew up. We use the oranges, lemons, limes, satsumas, and grapefruit from those citrus trees as much as possible at home and in our restaurants. This vinaigrette is great on any salad, especially those made with seafood or chicken.

Juice of 1 navel orange

Juice of 2 lemons

Juice of 1 lime

¼ cup honey

Pinch kosher salt

3 garlic cloves

3 green onions, chopped

¼ cup Steen's cane vinegar (substitute apple cider vinegar or unseasoned rice wine vinegar)

2 cups vegetable oil

Combine the juices, honey, salt, garlic, green onions, and vinegar in a blender or food processor and process to combine.

With the processor or blender running, stream in the oil through the feeding tube in the top until the dressing has emulsified. Store in the refrigerator for up to 7 days.

TAJIN VINAIGRETTE MAKES ¾ CUP

2 tablespoons Tajin seasoning

Kosher salt

Black pepper

¼ cup Steen's cane vinegar

½ cup vegetable oil

Combine the Tajin seasoning, salt and pepper to taste, and vinegar in a small bowl and whisk in the oil until it has emulsified. Store in the refrigerator for up to 7 days

BLACK PEPPER CAESAR DRESSING MAKES ABOUT 4 CUPS

4 large eggs

2 anchovy fillets

2 teaspoons black pepper

½ teaspoon Worcestershire sauce

1 tablespoon Italian flat-leaf parsley

Juice of 1 lemon

1 cup grated Parmesan cheese

½ cup peeled garlic cloves

2½ cups vegetable oil

Combine the eggs, anchovy fillets, pepper, Worcestershire sauce, parsley, lemon juice, Parmesan cheese, and garlic in a food processor or blender and blend on high to combine. With the processor or blender running, stream in the oil through the feeding tube at the top until fully incorporated and the dressing has emulsified. Store in the refrigerator for up to 6 days.

CREOLE RÉMOULADE MAKES 1 PINT

In New Orleans you will find some version of this sauce on every menu. It's creamy and a little spicy so it really works well with seafood.

3 tablespoons diced onion

3 tablespoons diced green bell pepper

1½ tablespoons hot sauce

2 cups mayonnaise

1 teaspoon prepared horseradish

4 tablespoons Creole mustard

1 teaspoon paprika

½ teaspoon celery salt

½ teaspoon Creole seasoning

Combine the onion, bell pepper, and hot sauce in a blender or food processor and pulse several times to purée.

Add the mayonnaise, horseradish, mustard, paprika, celery salt, and Creole seasoning and process the mixture to blend.

Chill for 6 to 8 hours or overnight before using. Store in the refrigerator for up to 5 days.

GREEN RÉMOULADE MAKES 1¼ CUPS

This bright, herbal sauce is great on anything—chilled or fried seafood, chicken, vegetables, or as a sandwich spread.

1 cup mayonnaise

2 tablespoons Creole mustard

2 tablespoons prepared horseradish

3 green onions, green parts only, sliced

1 tablespoon chopped Italian flat-leaf parsley

1 to 2 teaspoons freshly squeezed lemon juice

Kosher salt

Black pepper

Creole seasoning

Combine the mayonnaise, mustard, horseradish, green onions, and parsley in a blender and process on high until just combined.

While the blender is running, drizzle 1 teaspoon of the lemon juice through the feeder tube at the top of the blender until the sauce is the consistency of ranch dressing. Add more lemon juice if needed. Season with salt, pepper, and Creole seasoning to taste. Store in the refrigerator for up to 6 days.

CHICKEN STOCK MAKES 1 GALLON

2 pounds chicken bones, raw or roasted (roasted bones will result in a darker stock)

2 medium onions, coarsely chopped

2 carrots, peeled and coarsely chopped

2 stalks celery, coarsely chopped

1 medium head garlic, cut in half crosswise

1 tablespoon whole black peppercorns

Place the chicken bones in a stockpot set over low heat. Add the onions, carrots, celery, garlic, peppercorns, and 1 gallon cold water and cook at a very low simmer (do not boil) for a minimum of 3 hours.

Cool and strain the stock. Discard the solids. Can freeze in an airtight container for 2 months, or keep in the refrigerator for up to 5 days.

SHRIMP STOCK MAKES 1 GALLON

1 pound shrimp shells and heads

2 medium onions, coarsely chopped

2 stalks celery, coarsely chopped

1 medium head garlic, cut in half crosswise

Combine the shrimp heads and shells in a stockpot set over very low heat. Add the onions, celery, garlic, and 1 gallon cold water and cook at a very low simmer (do not boil) for 1 hour. Cool and strain the stock. Discard the solids. Can freeze in an airtight container for 2 months, or keep in the refrigerator for up to 5 days.

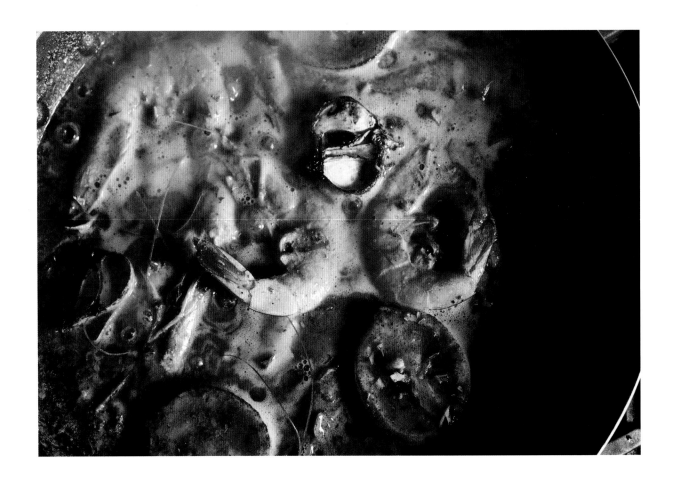

BEEF STOCK MAKES 1 GALLON

1 pound stew meat and/or beef scraps, cut into 2-inch chunks

2 onions, chopped

2 carrots, peeled and chopped

Blended oil or vegetable oil

5 pounds meaty beef bones, including some knuckle bones

2 stalks celery, chopped

3 garlic cloves, unpeeled

2 sprigs Italian flat-leaf parsley

2 bay leaves

10 peppercorns

Preheat the oven to 400°F.

Combine the stew meat/scraps, onions, and carrots in a roasting pan. Add a little oil and toss to coat. Add the bones.

Roast the meat, vegetables, and bones, turning the bones and meat pieces halfway through, for about 45 minutes, or until evenly browned. Take care not to burn the bones.

Transfer the contents of the roasting pan to a large stockpot and cover with 1 gallon cold water. Set the heat to low.

Place the roasting pan on the stovetop over medium-low heat. Slowly pour ½ cup of hot water in the pan and use a wooden spoon to scrape up the browned bits stuck to the bottom of the pan. Add this liquid to the stockpot.

Add the celery, garlic, parsley, bay leaves, and peppercorns to the stockpot and simmer for at least 6 hours, ideally 8 hours, occasionally skimming the surface for impurities. Never allow the stock to boil.

Strain the stock, chill, and skim off the layer of fat from the top. Can freeze in an airtight container for 2 months, or keep in the refrigerator for up to 5 days.

VEAL STOCK MAKES 1 GALLON

10 pounds veal bones

3 carrots, peeled and chopped

3 large onions, chopped

3 stalks celery, chopped

2 tablespoons tomato paste

2 cups dry white wine

2 heads garlic, cut in half crosswise

2 bay leaves

1 tablespoon black peppercorns

3 sprigs Italian flat-leaf parsley

Preheat oven to 400°F.

Roast the veal bones in a large roasting pan until they begin to brown, 1 to 1½ hours.

Add the carrots, onions, celery, and tomato paste, mix well, and continue roasting until the vegetables and bones are well-browned, about 40 minutes.

Transfer the bones and vegetables to a large stockpot.

Do not wash or wipe the roasting pan. Set the roasting pan over medium heat, add the wine, and deglaze the pan by scraping up the browned bits on the bottom. Simmer for about 1 minute, then add this liquid to stockpot.

Add the garlic, bay leaves, peppercorns, parsley, and 1 gallon cold water to the stockpot and simmer over low heat, skimming occasionally to remove impurities, for 8 hours. Never allow the stock to boil.

Strain the stock, chill, and skim off the layer of fat from the top. Can freeze in an airtight container for up to 2 months, or keep in the refrigerator for up to 5 days.

CHICKEN DREDGE MAKES ABOUT 2¼ CUPS

1 cup all-purpose flour

1 cup cornstarch

1 tablespoon celery salt

1 teaspoon white pepper

1 teaspoon black pepper

1 tablespoon granulated garlic

1 tablespoon onion powder

2 tablespoons Creole
   seasoning

Combine the flour, cornstarch, celery salt, peppers, garlic, onion powder, and Creole seasoning in a bowl and mix well. Store in an airtight container at room temperature for up to 4 weeks.

SEAFOOD DREDGE MAKES 3¼ CUPS

2 cups all-purpose flour

1 cup yellow cornmeal

¼ cup Creole seasoning

Combine the flour, cornmeal, and Creole seasoning in a bowl and mix well. Store in an airtight container at room temperature for up to 4 weeks.

INDEX

METRIC CONVERSION CHART

Volume Measurements		Weight Measurements		Temperature	
U.S.	Metric	U.S.	Metric	Fahrenheit	Celsius
1 teaspoon	5 ml	½ ounce	15 g	250	120
1 tablespoon	15 ml	1 ounce	30 g	300	150
¼ cup	60 ml	3 ounces	80 g	325	160
⅓ cup	80 ml	4 ounces	115 g	350	175
½ cup	125 ml	8 ounces	225 g	375	190
⅔ cup	160 ml	12 ounces	340 g	400	200
¾ cup	180 ml	1 pound	450 g	425	220
1 cup	250 ml	2¼ pounds	1 kg	450	230

ABOUT THE AUTHOR

Eric Cook, a native of New Orleans, Louisiana, is a combat veteran who served six years in the United States Marine Corps. With training from the John Folse Culinary Institute, he began his culinary career at Brennan's in the French Quarter, where he studied under Chef Mike Roussel. Cook joined the team at Commander's Palace as sous-chef and chef de partie. He has also worked as a private chef, executive banquet chef, and research and development consultant for several national restaurants. His career has taken him through some of the finest restaurants in New Orleans, and he has served as Executive Chef for the National WWII Museum's American Sector, Dickie Brennan's Bourbon House, Tommy's Cuisine, and N.O.S.H.

In 2018, Cook opened his first restaurant, Gris-Gris, in the Lower Garden District of New Orleans. Using his years of experience in fine dining, he wanted to create a menu with refined Southern cuisine and local favorites served in a relaxed atmosphere. That first year, Gris-Gris was named *Eater Magazine* Reader's Choice for both Restaurant and

Chef of the Year in addition to a series of local awards for best restaurant, best gumbo, best brunch, and best happy hour.

Cook opened his second restaurant, Saint John, in the French Quarter just after Hurricane Ida in 2021. Specializing in "haute Creole cuisine," Saint John showcases the evolution of true Creole cuisine dating back to the eighteenth century, and once again presents local cuisine in an elevated, yet approachable way. The menu reflects influences from the melting pot of cultures that lent flavors, ingredients, and cooking styles to the city.

In his career, Cook has worked on television shows such as *Top Chef New Orleans* and *Off the Menu, After Hours with Daniel Boulud*. Most recently he was featured on *Gordon Ramsay's: Uncharted*. Cook and his restaurants have been featured in magazines such as *Bon Appétit*, *Country Roads*, *Saveur*, *Flavor & The Menu*, *Plate Magazine*, and *Louisiana Cookin'*. He represented Commander's Palace at the James Beard House "Wild About Wild American Shrimp" event in New York City, and at the grand opening of the Southern Food and Beverage Museum (SoFAB) in New Orleans. He has been honored to cook for the NFL Hall of Fame, the U.S. Marine Corps Ball and U.S. Navy Ball, and private dinners for the Sergeant Major of the United States Marine Corps and the Vice Admiral of the Navy Reserve. One of his most memorable experiences was a special dinner for President George W. Bush, the President of Mexico, and the Prime Minister of Canada.

In addition to being an outspoken representative for his hometown, its culture, and its cuisine, Cook frequently volunteers for events such as the Café Hope Mentor Program, Edible Schoolyard New Orleans, NOCHI Culinary School, St. Michael's Chef's Charity, Stan Brock's Black & Gold Foundation, and many schools and charitable organizations. In 2019 he was named a "Culinary Legend" at the ACF Best Chefs of Louisiana.

Cook continues to advocate for the U.S. military and veterans. He is a member of the Veterans of Foreign Wars and founder of the First to Fight Foundation, which assists veterans in the transition from military to civilian life. Cook is an active volunteer for organizations such as Wounded Warriors, the Legacy Foundation, Disposable Heroes Project, We Heart Veterans, and the American Red Cross.

In his personal time, Cook relaxes by gardening at home and going fishing as often as possible. He enjoys traveling with his wife, rock concerts with his daughter, and cooking for his three dogs, Siouxsie Sioux, Cleopatra, and Sid Vicious.